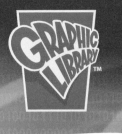

Graphic Library

Graphic Science

Understanding Global Warming with Max Axiom Super Scientist

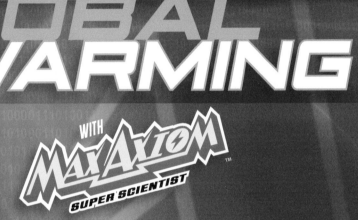

An Augmented Reading Science Experience

by Agnieszka Biskup | illustrated by Cynthia Martin and Bill Anderson

Consultant:
Joseph M. Moran, PhD
Associate Director, Education Program
American Meteorological Society, Washington, D.C.

CAPSTONE PRESS
a capstone imprint

Graphic Library is published by Capstone Press,
1710 Roe Crest Drive, North Mankato, Minnesota 56003.
www.capstonepub.com

Library of Congress Cataloging-in-Publication Data is available on the Library of
Congress website.
ISBN: 978-1-5435-2953-1 (library binding)
ISBN: 978-1-5435-2964-7 (paperback)
ISBN: 978-1-5435-2974-6 (eBook PDF)

Summary: In graphic novel format, follows the adventures of Max Axiom as he
explains the science behind global warming.

Art Director and Designer
Bob Lentz and Thomas Emery

Colorist
Matt Webb

Cover Artist
Tod Smith

Editor
Donald Lemke

Photo Credits
Capstone Studio/Karon Dubke: 29; NASA: 15; Shutterstock/
Margaud: 21

This is a Capstone 4D book!

Want fun videos that go with this book?

Just visit www.capstone4d.com

Use this password

global.29531

Printed in the United States   6000

TABLE OF CONTENTS

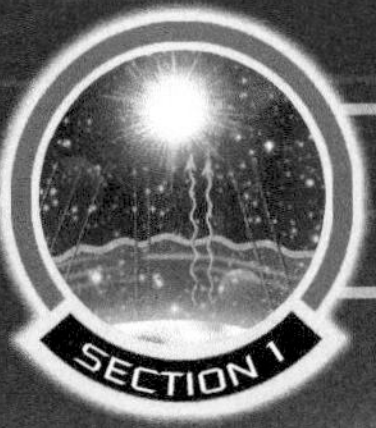
SECTION 1

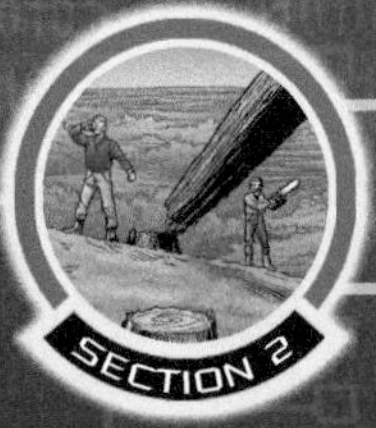
SECTION 2

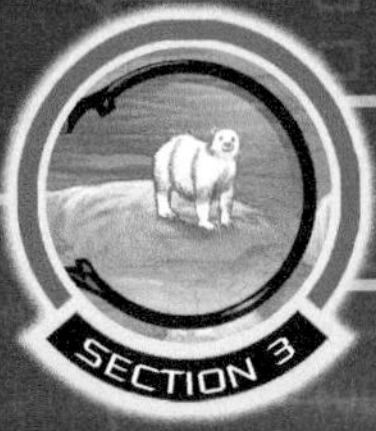
SECTION 3

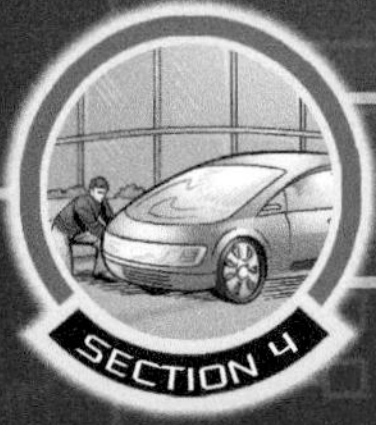
SECTION 4

SECTION 1 THE GREENHOUSE EFFECT

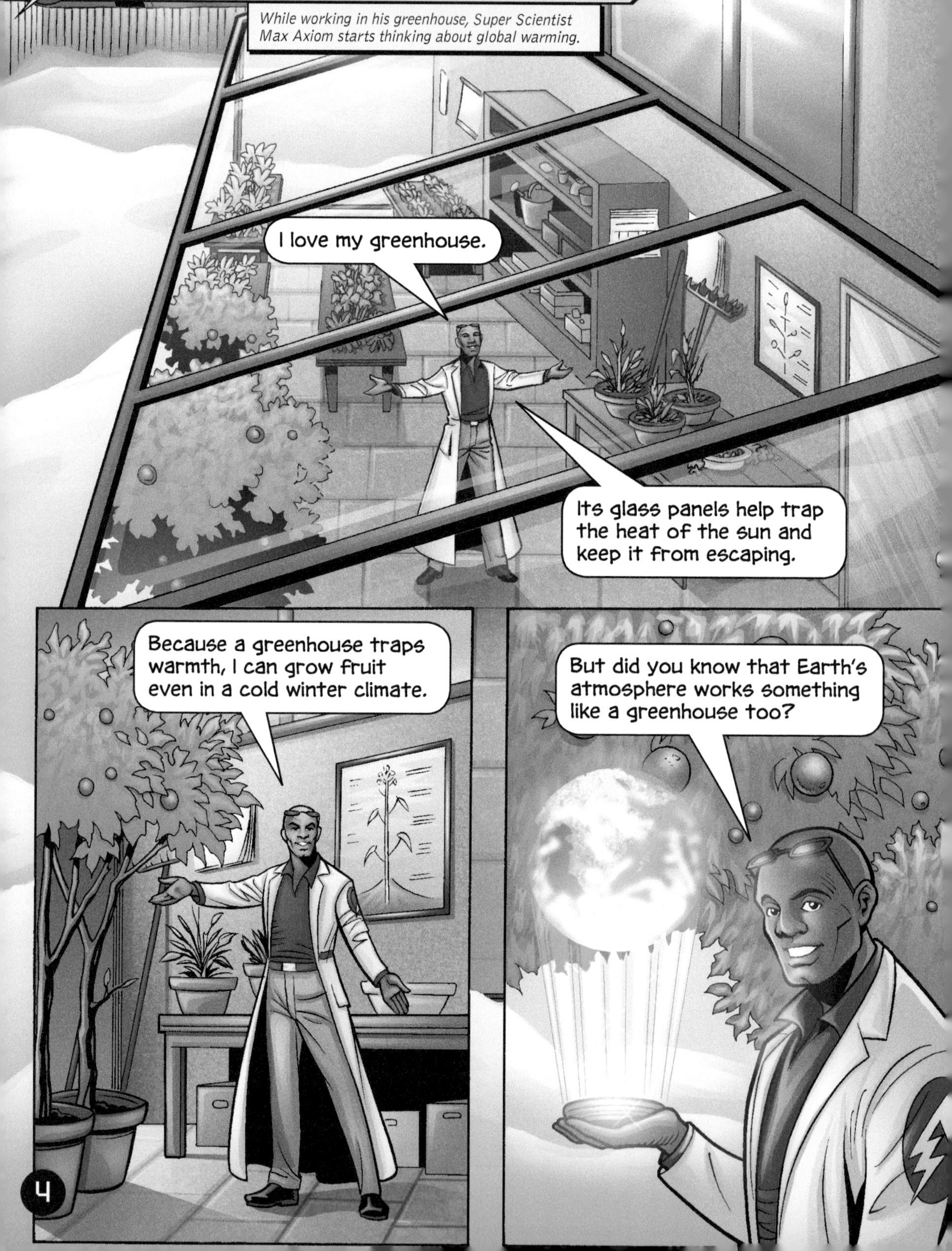
While working in his greenhouse, Super Scientist Max Axiom starts thinking about global warming.
I love my greenhouse.
Its glass panels help trap the heat of the sun and keep it from escaping.
Because a greenhouse traps warmth, I can grow fruit even in a cold winter climate.
But did you know that Earth's atmosphere works something like a greenhouse too?

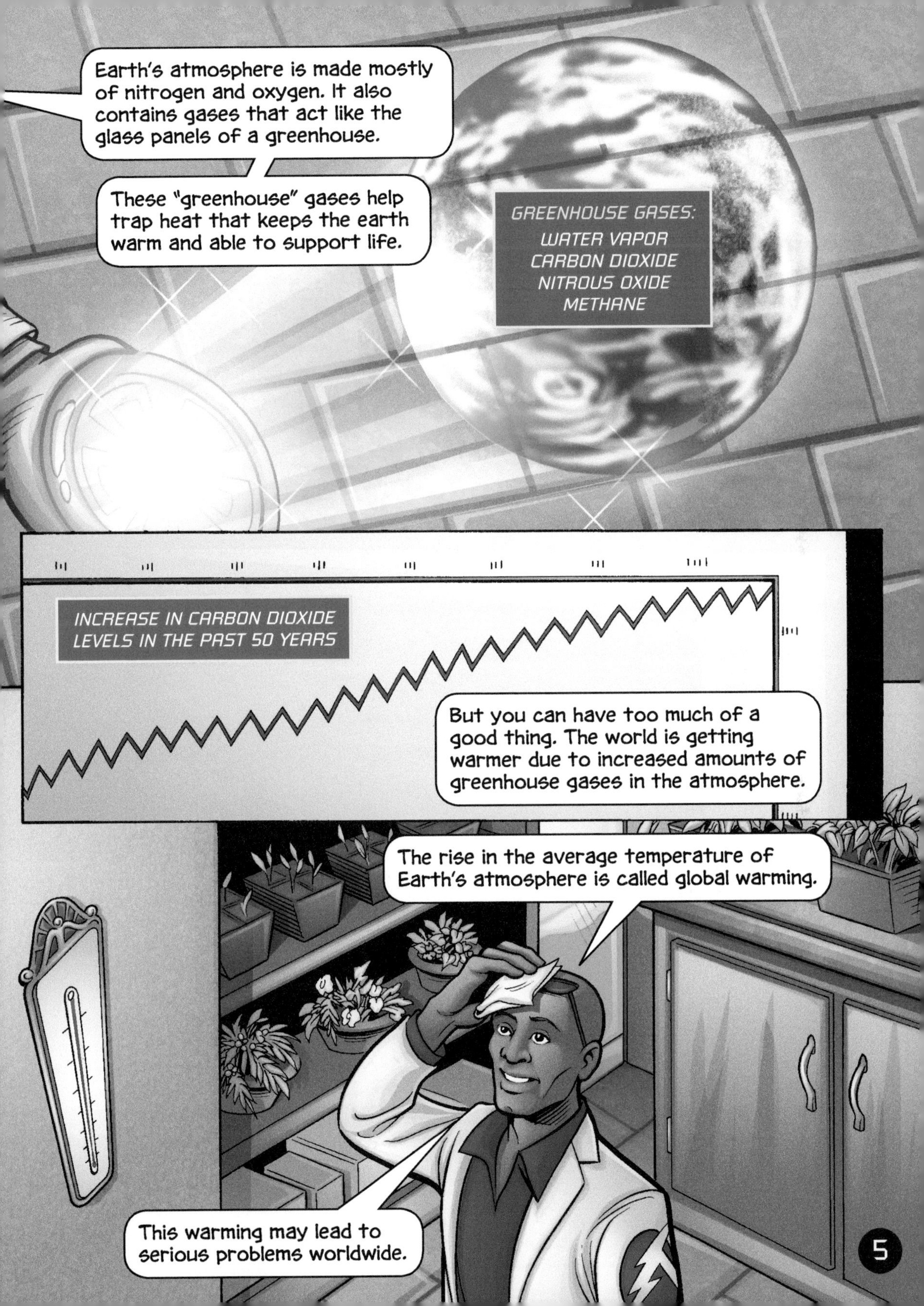

Earth's atmosphere is made mostly of nitrogen and oxygen. It also contains gases that act like the glass panels of a greenhouse.
These "greenhouse" gases help trap heat that keeps the earth warm and able to support life.
GREENHOUSE GASES:
WATER VAPOR
CARBON DIOXIDE
NITROUS OXIDE
METHANE
INCREASE IN CARBON DIOXIDE LEVELS IN THE PAST 50 YEARS
But you can have too much of a good thing. The world is getting warmer due to increased amounts of greenhouse gases in the atmosphere.
The rise in the average temperature of Earth's atmosphere is called global warming.
This warming may lead to serious problems worldwide.

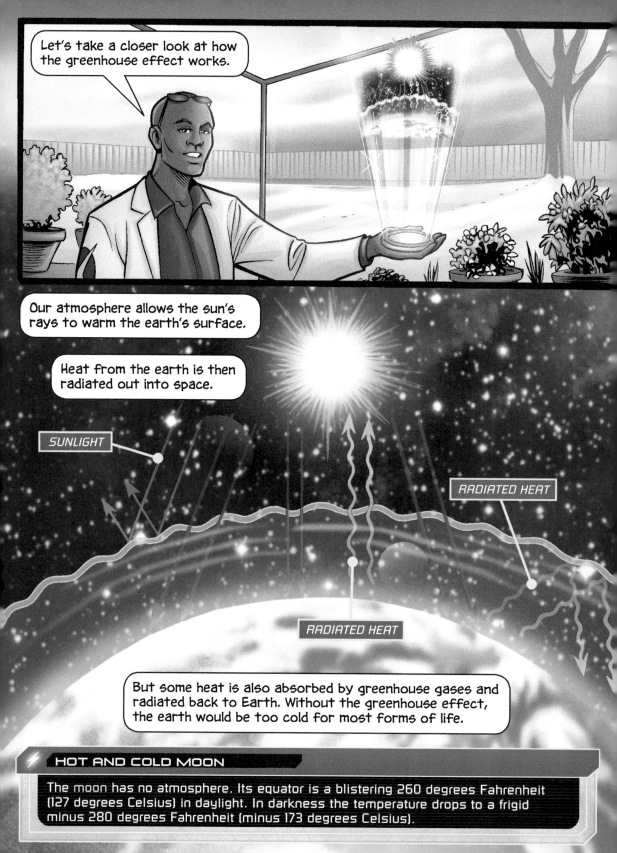

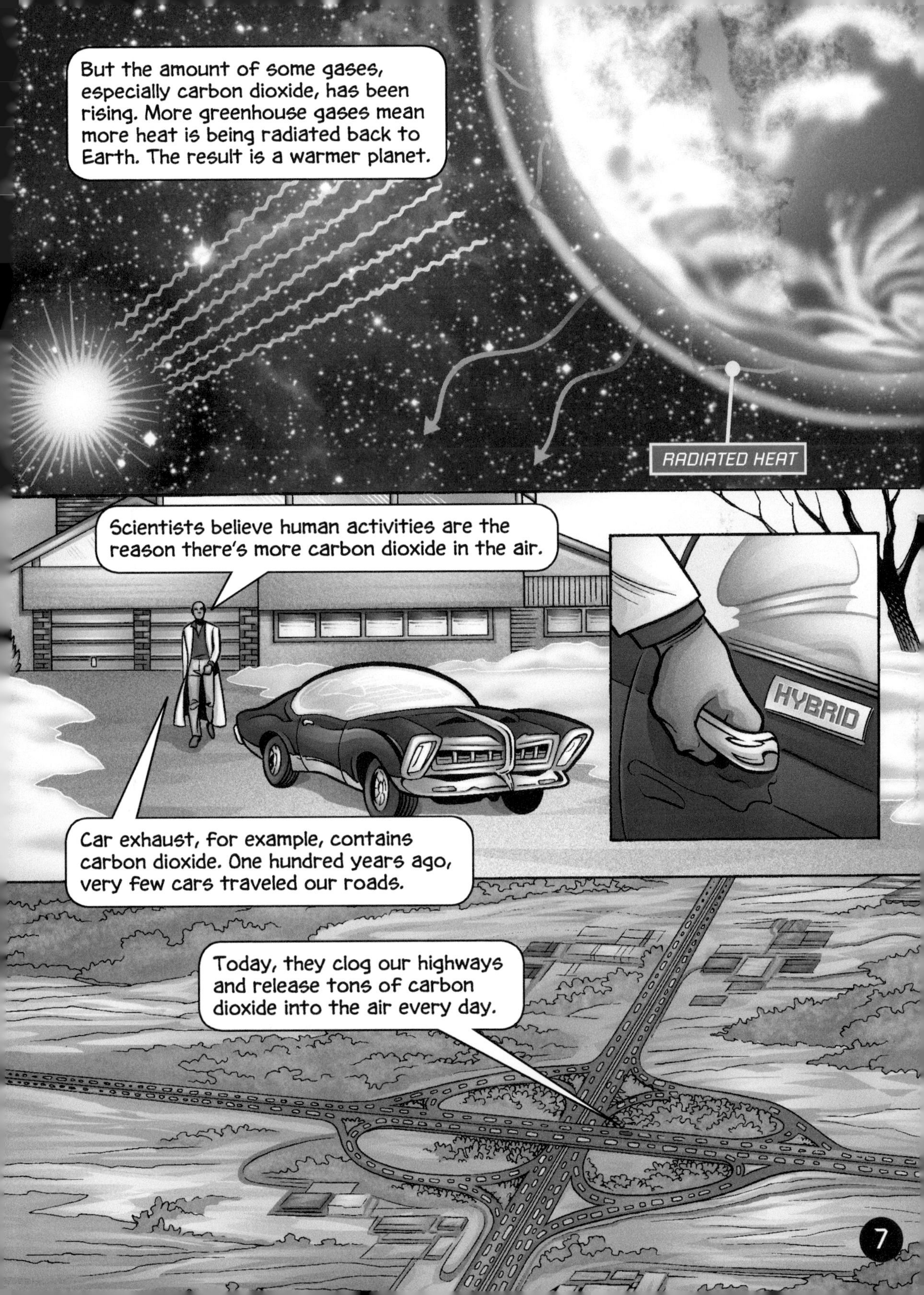

But the amount of some gases, especially carbon dioxide, has been rising. More greenhouse gases mean more heat is being radiated back to Earth. The result is a warmer planet.
RADIATED HEAT
Scientists believe human activities are the reason there's more carbon dioxide in the air.
HYBRID
Car exhaust, for example, contains carbon dioxide. One hundred years ago, very few cars traveled our roads.
Today, they clog our highways and release tons of carbon dioxide into the air every day.

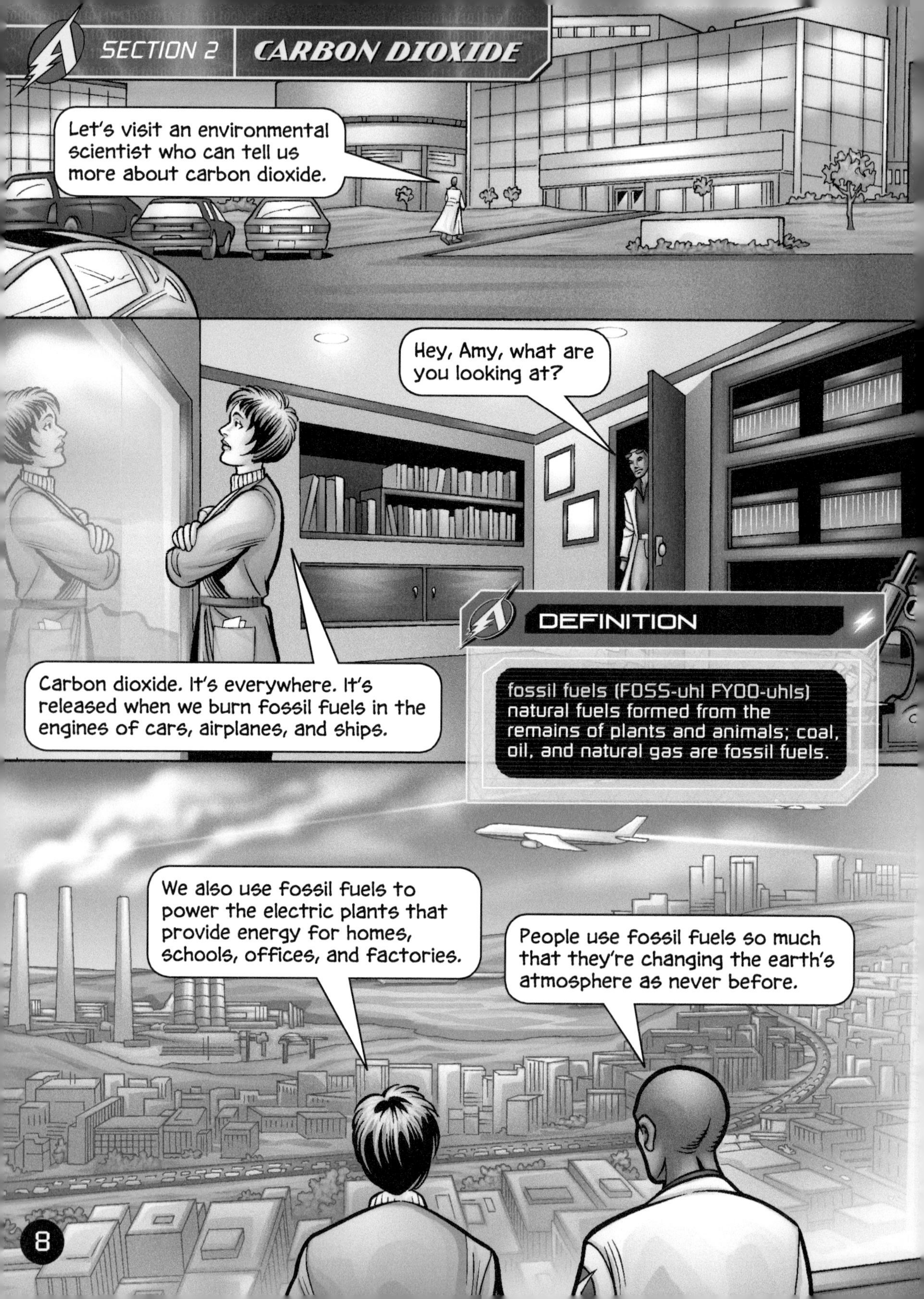
SECTION 2
CARBON DIOXIDE
Let's visit an environmental scientist who can tell us more about carbon dioxide.
Hey, Amy, what are you looking at?
Carbon dioxide. It's everywhere. It's released when we burn fossil fuels in the engines of cars, airplanes, and ships.
DEFINITION
fossil fuels (FOSS-uhl FYOO-uhls) natural fuels formed from the remains of plants and animals; coal, oil, and natural gas are fossil fuels.
We also use fossil fuels to power the electric plants that provide energy for homes, schools, offices, and factories.
People use fossil fuels so much that they're changing the earth's atmosphere as never before.

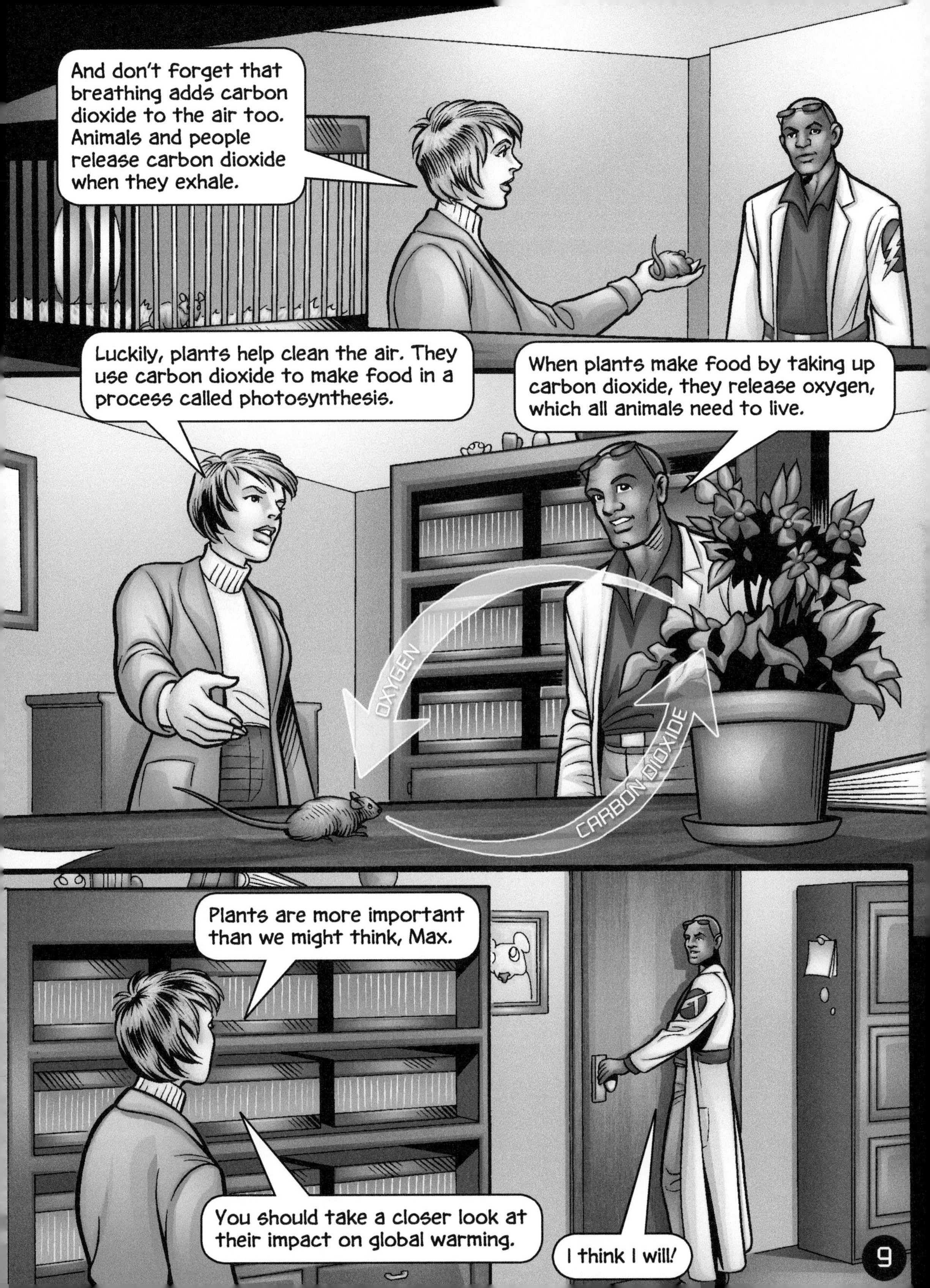
And don't forget that breathing adds carbon dioxide to the air too. Animals and people release carbon dioxide when they exhale.
Luckily, plants help clean the air. They use carbon dioxide to make food in a process called photosynthesis.
When plants make food by taking up carbon dioxide, they release oxygen, which all animals need to live.
OXYGEN
CARBON DIOXIDE
Plants are more important than we might think, Max.
You should take a closer look at their impact on global warming.
I think I will!

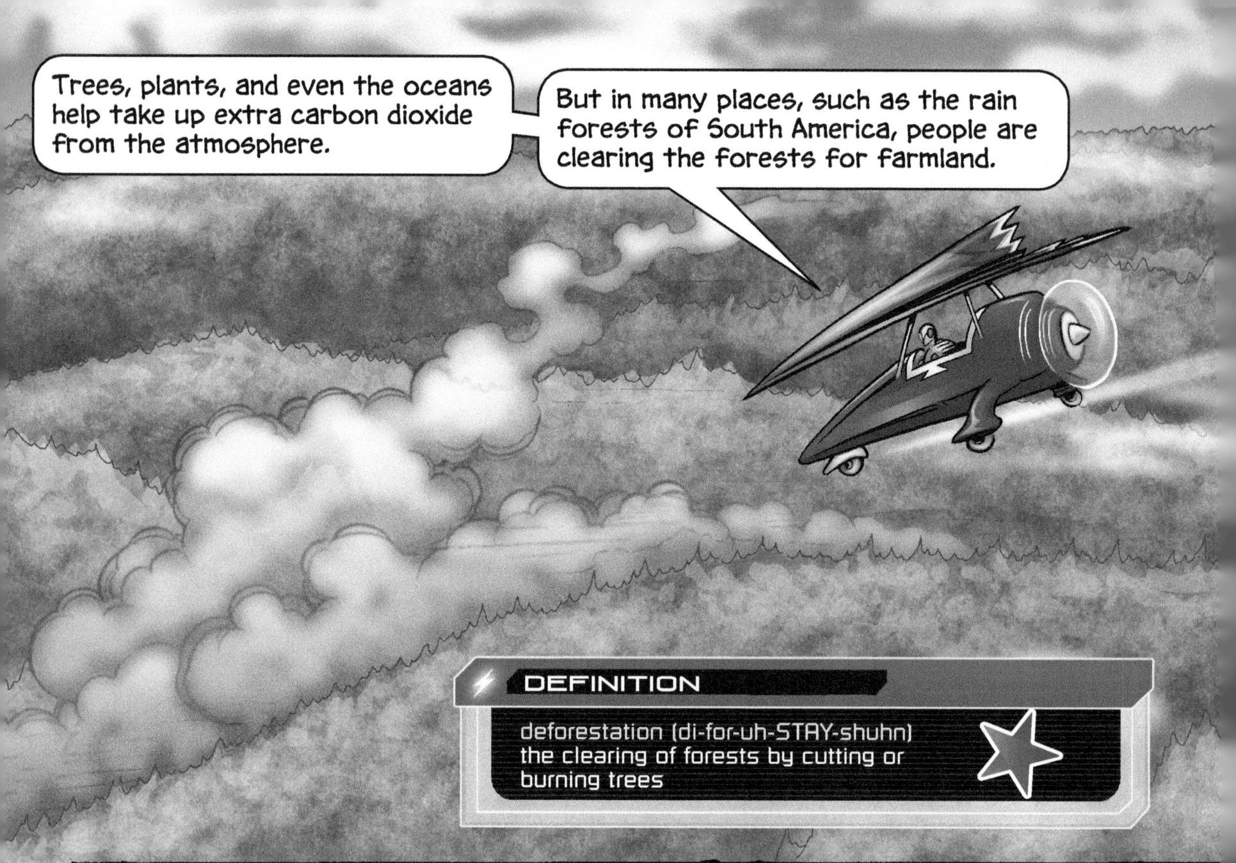
Trees, plants, and even the oceans help take up extra carbon dioxide from the atmosphere.
But in many places, such as the rain forests of South America, people are clearing the forests for farmland.

DEFINITION

deforestation (di-for-uh-STAY-shuhn)
the clearing of forests by cutting or burning trees

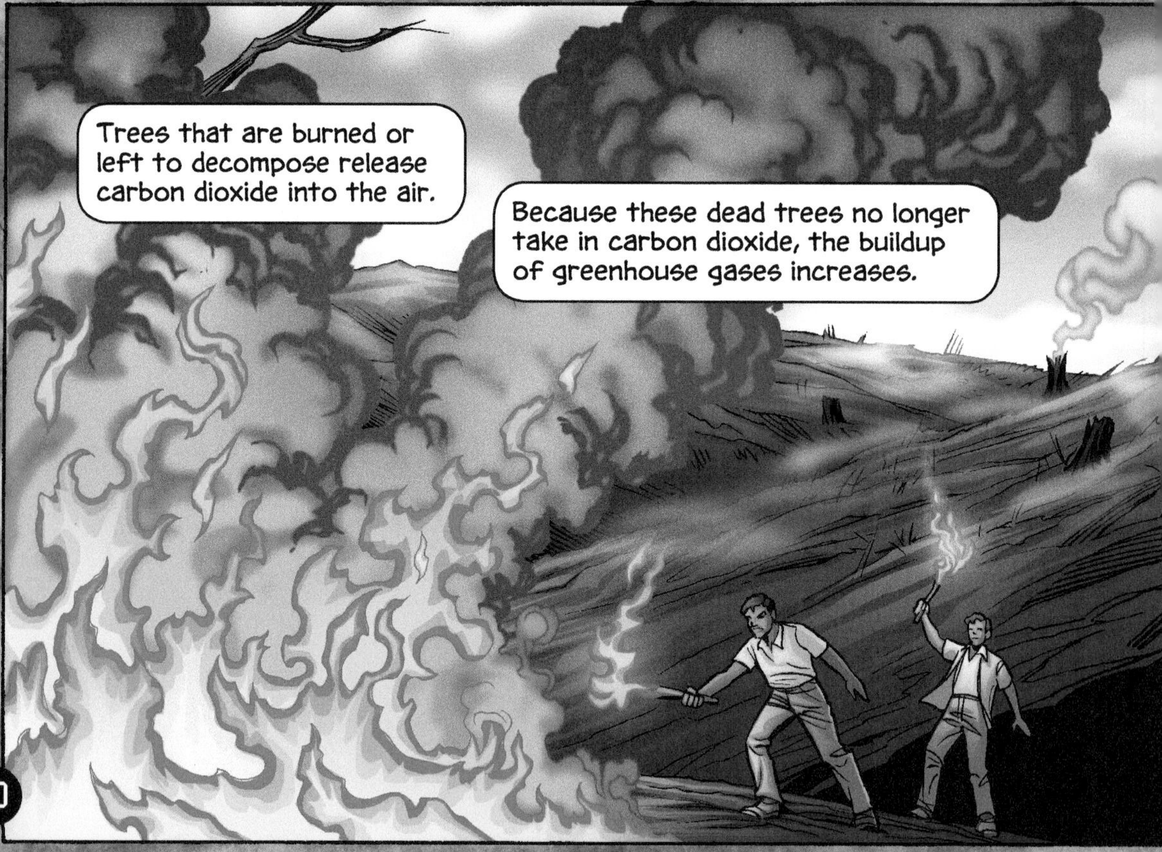
Trees that are burned or left to decompose release carbon dioxide into the air.
Because these dead trees no longer take in carbon dioxide, the buildup of greenhouse gases increases.

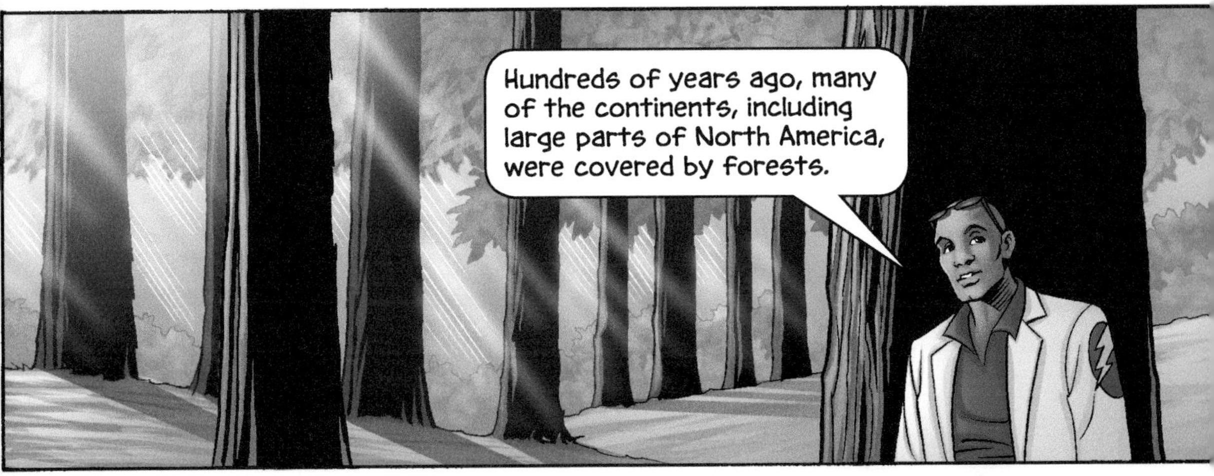
Hundreds of years ago, many of the continents, including large parts of North America, were covered by forests.

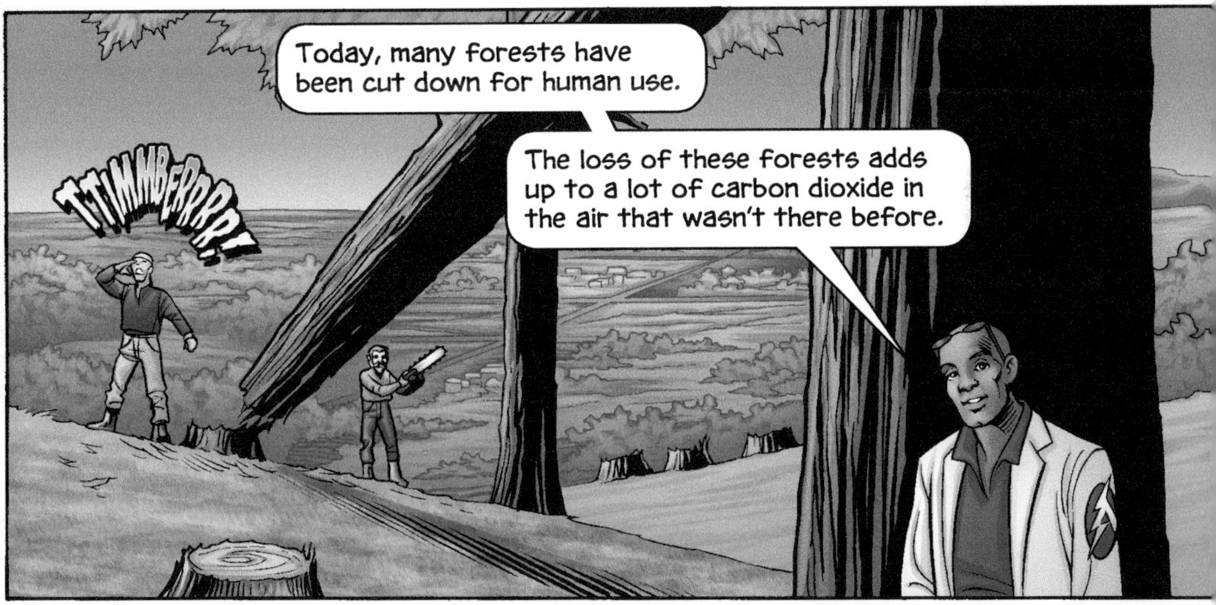
Today, many forests have been cut down for human use.
TTIMMBERRRR!
The loss of these forests adds up to a lot of carbon dioxide in the air that wasn't there before.

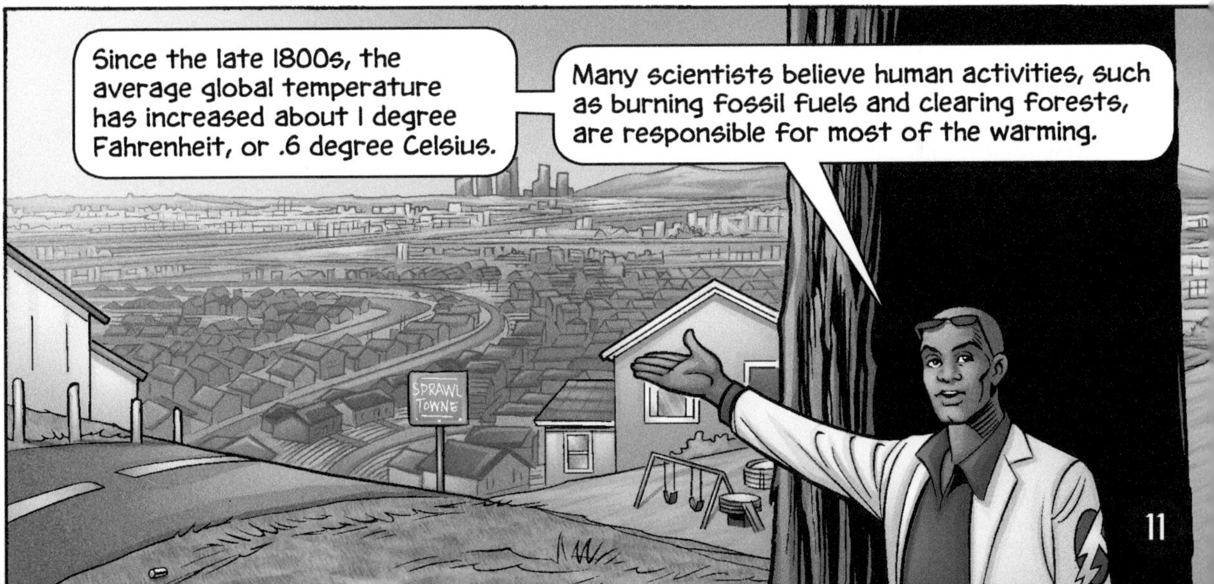
Since the late 1800s, the average global temperature has increased about 1 degree Fahrenheit, or .6 degree Celsius.
Many scientists believe human activities, such as burning fossil fuels and clearing forests, are responsible for most of the warming.
SPRAWL TOWNE

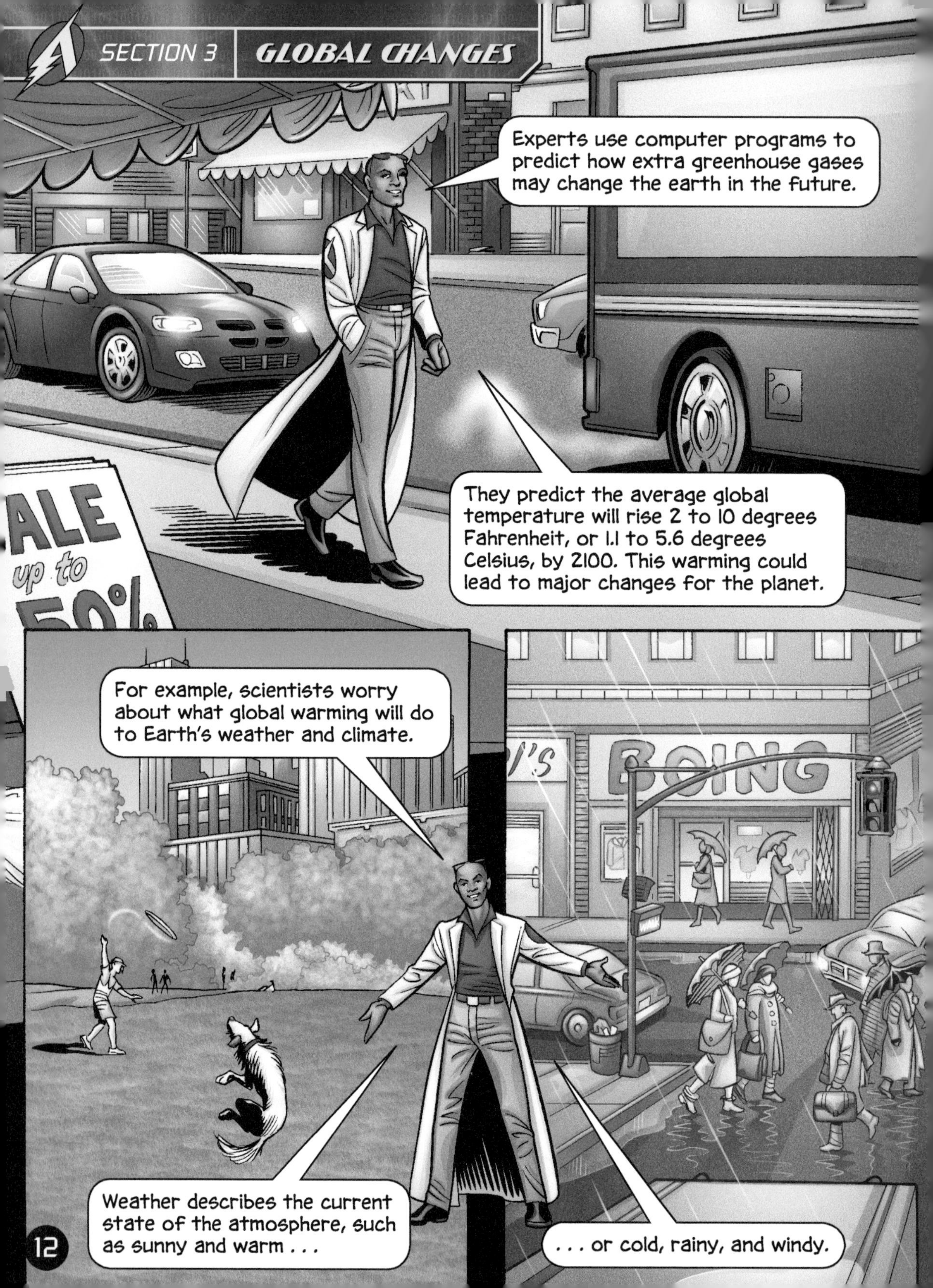
Experts use computer programs to predict how extra greenhouse gases may change the earth in the future.
They predict the average global temperature will rise 2 to 10 degrees Fahrenheit, or 1.1 to 5.6 degrees Celsius, by 2100. This warming could lead to major changes for the planet.
ALE up to 50%
For example, scientists worry about what global warming will do to Earth's weather and climate.
BOING
Weather describes the current state of the atmosphere, such as sunny and warm . . .
. . . or cold, rainy, and windy.

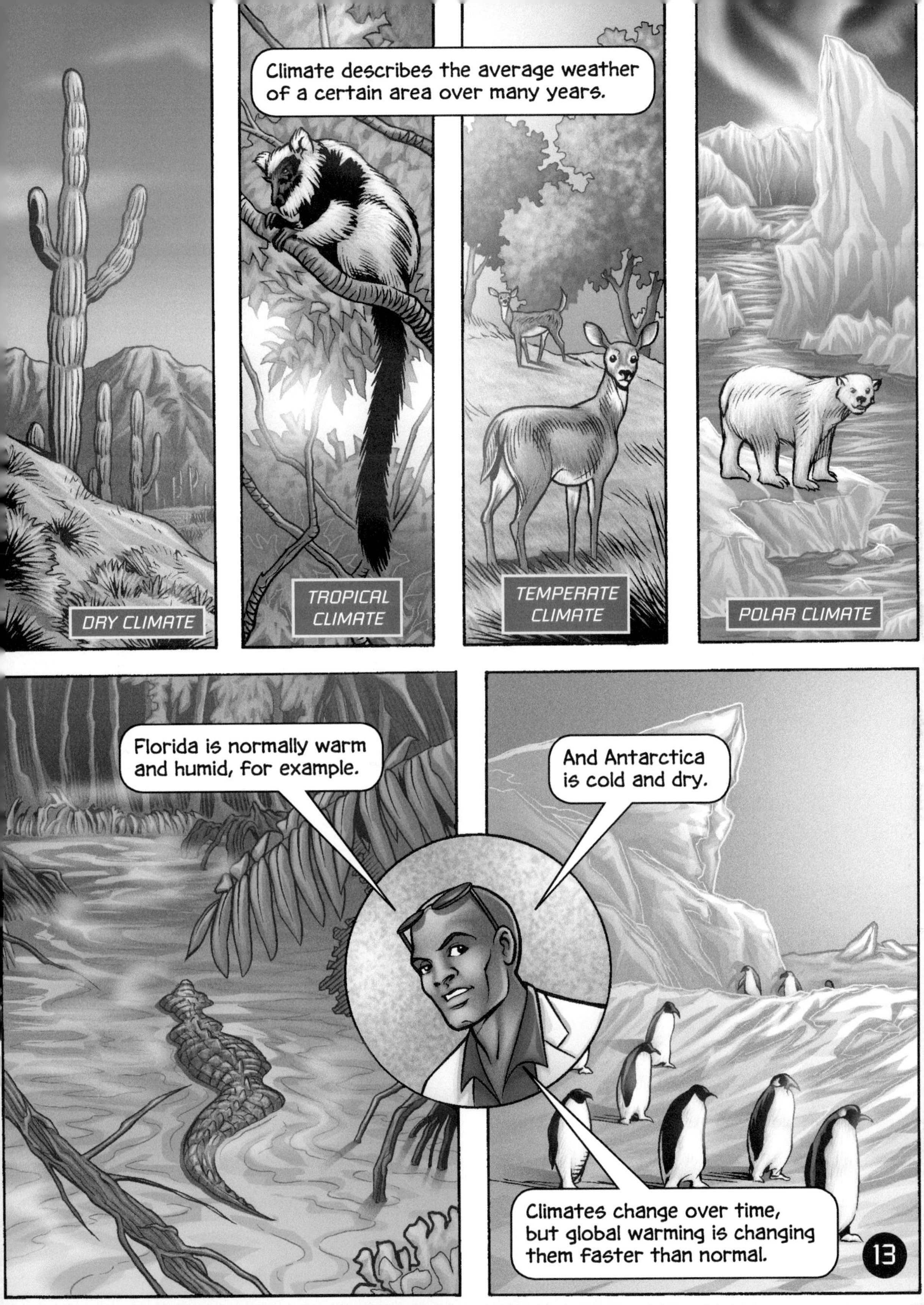
Climate describes the average weather of a certain area over many years.
DRY CLIMATE
TROPICAL CLIMATE
TEMPERATE CLIMATE
POLAR CLIMATE
Florida is normally warm and humid, for example.
And Antarctica is cold and dry.
Climates change over time, but global warming is changing them faster than normal.

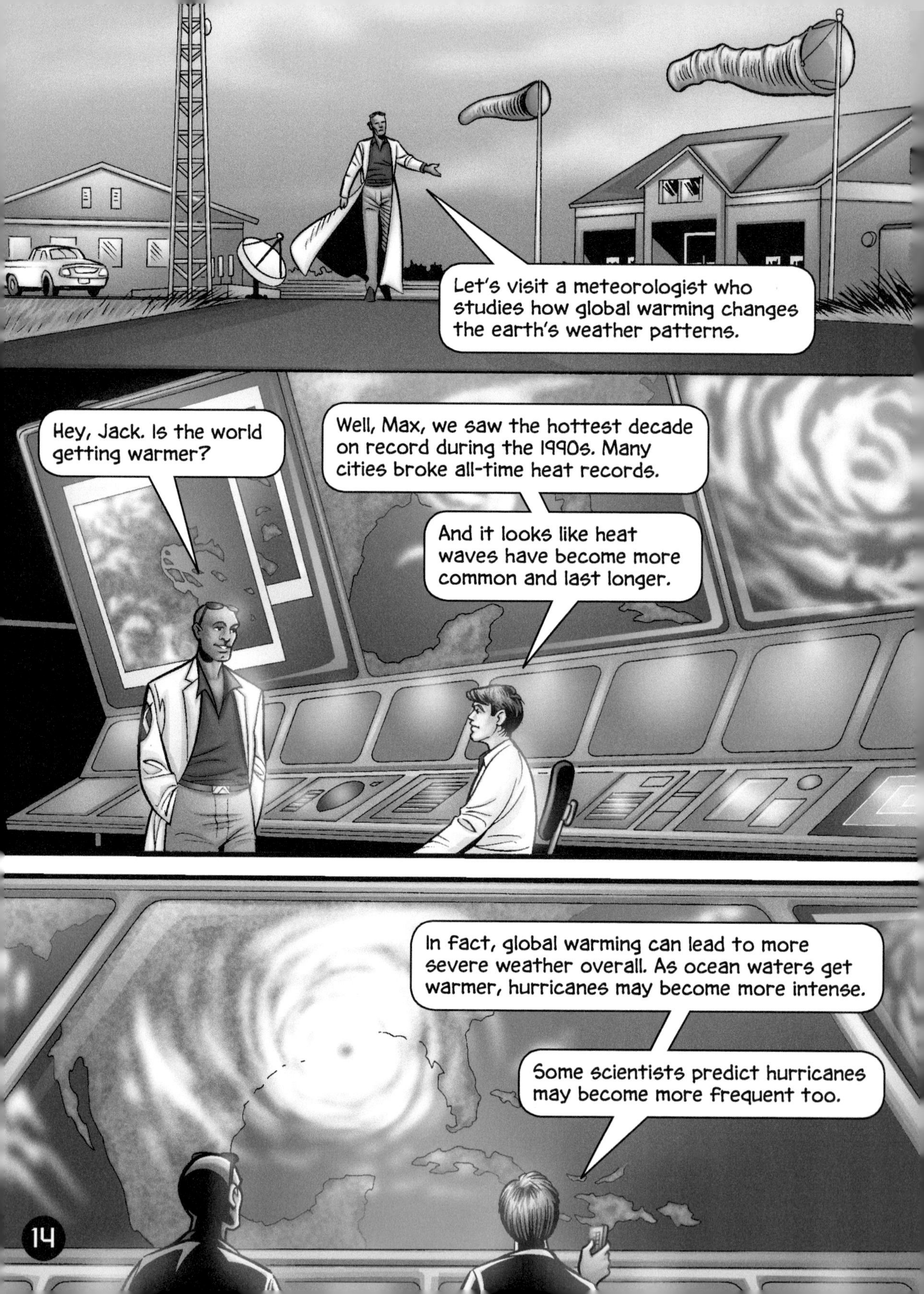
Let's visit a meteorologist who studies how global warming changes the earth's weather patterns.
Hey, Jack. Is the world getting warmer?
Well, Max, we saw the hottest decade on record during the 1990s. Many cities broke all-time heat records.
And it looks like heat waves have become more common and last longer.
In fact, global warming can lead to more severe weather overall. As ocean waters get warmer, hurricanes may become more intense.
Some scientists predict hurricanes may become more frequent too.

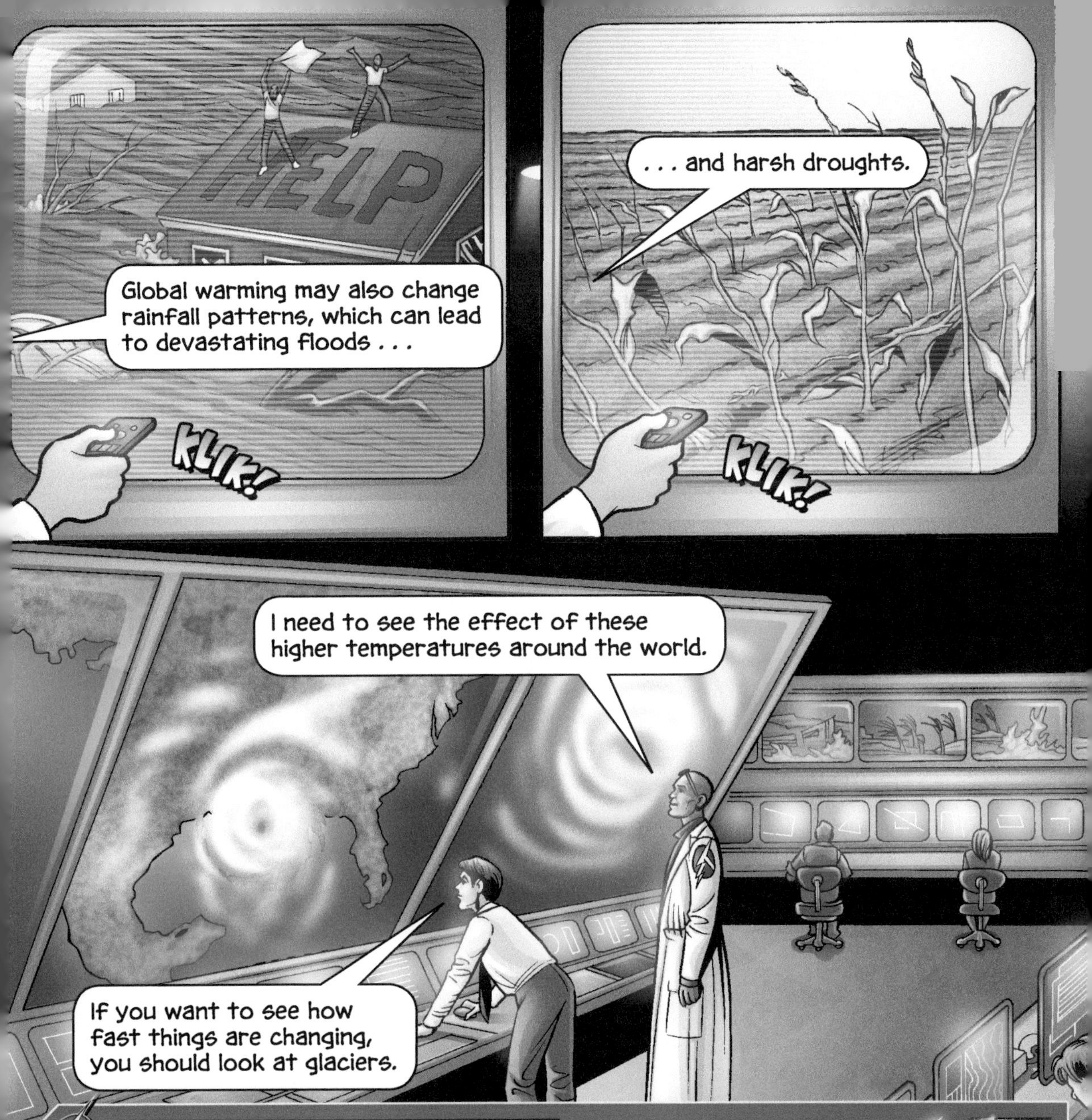
HELP
Global warming may also change rainfall patterns, which can lead to devastating floods . . .
KLIK!
. . . and harsh droughts.
KLIK!
I need to see the effect of these higher temperatures around the world.
If you want to see how fast things are changing, you should look at glaciers.

RECORD HURRICANES

ACCESS GRANTED: MAX AXIOM

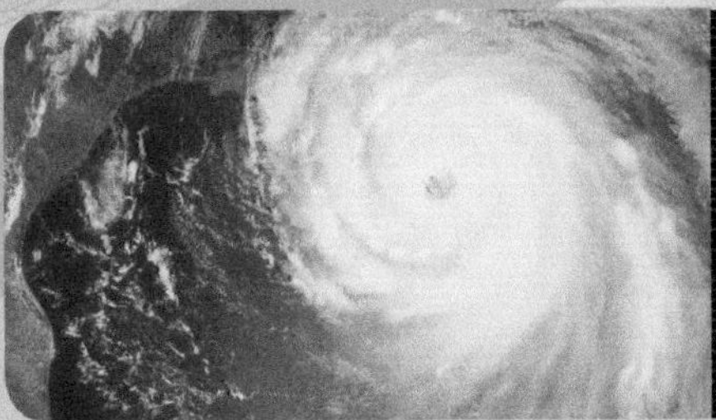

The 2005 Atlantic hurricane season set a new record with 27 named hurricanes and tropical storms. Hurricane Katrina devastated New Orleans in August 2005. It was one of the costliest and deadliest storms ever to hit the United States.

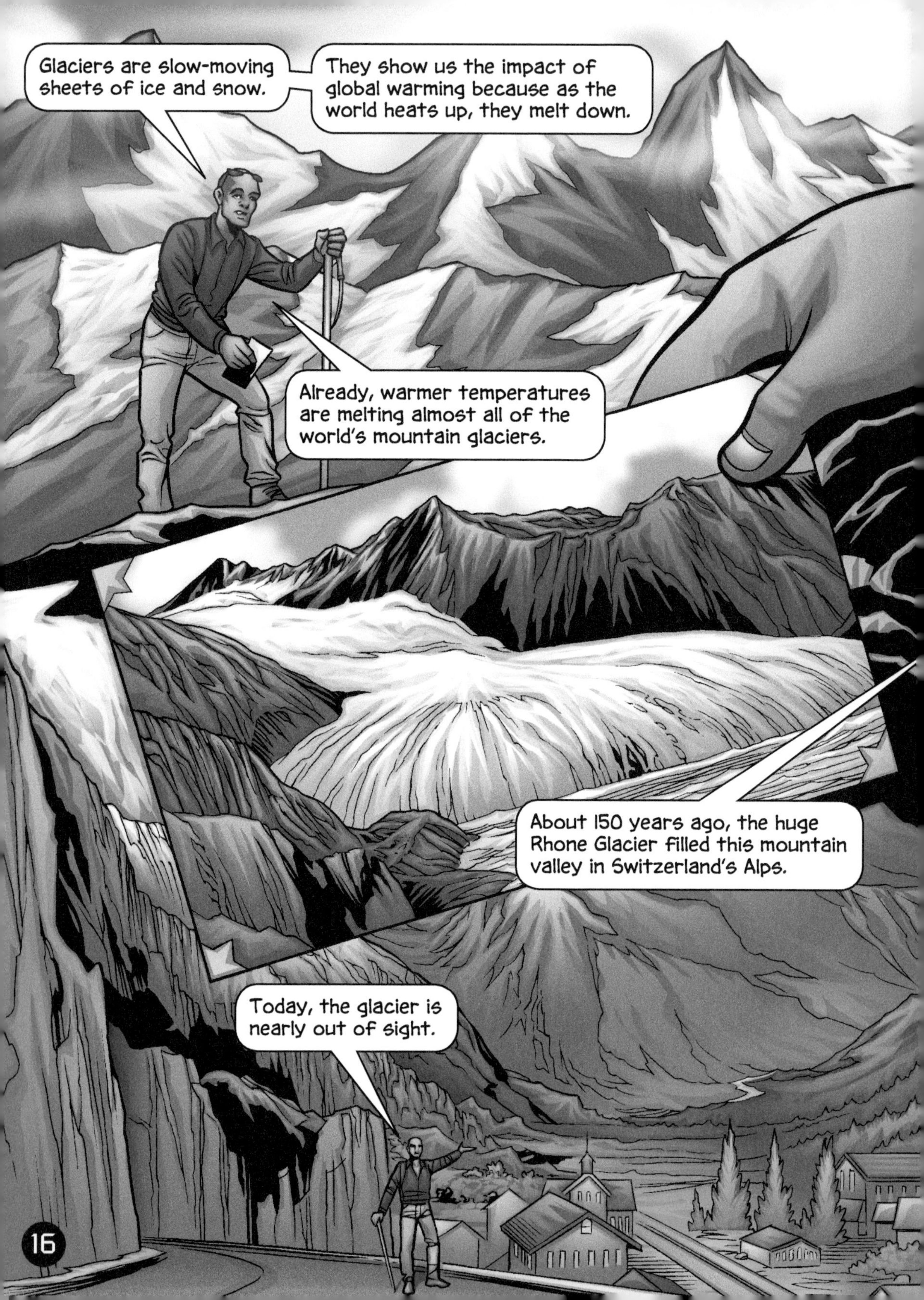

Glaciers are slow-moving sheets of ice and snow.
They show us the impact of global warming because as the world heats up, they melt down.
Already, warmer temperatures are melting almost all of the world's mountain glaciers.
About 150 years ago, the huge Rhone Glacier filled this mountain valley in Switzerland's Alps.
Today, the glacier is nearly out of sight.

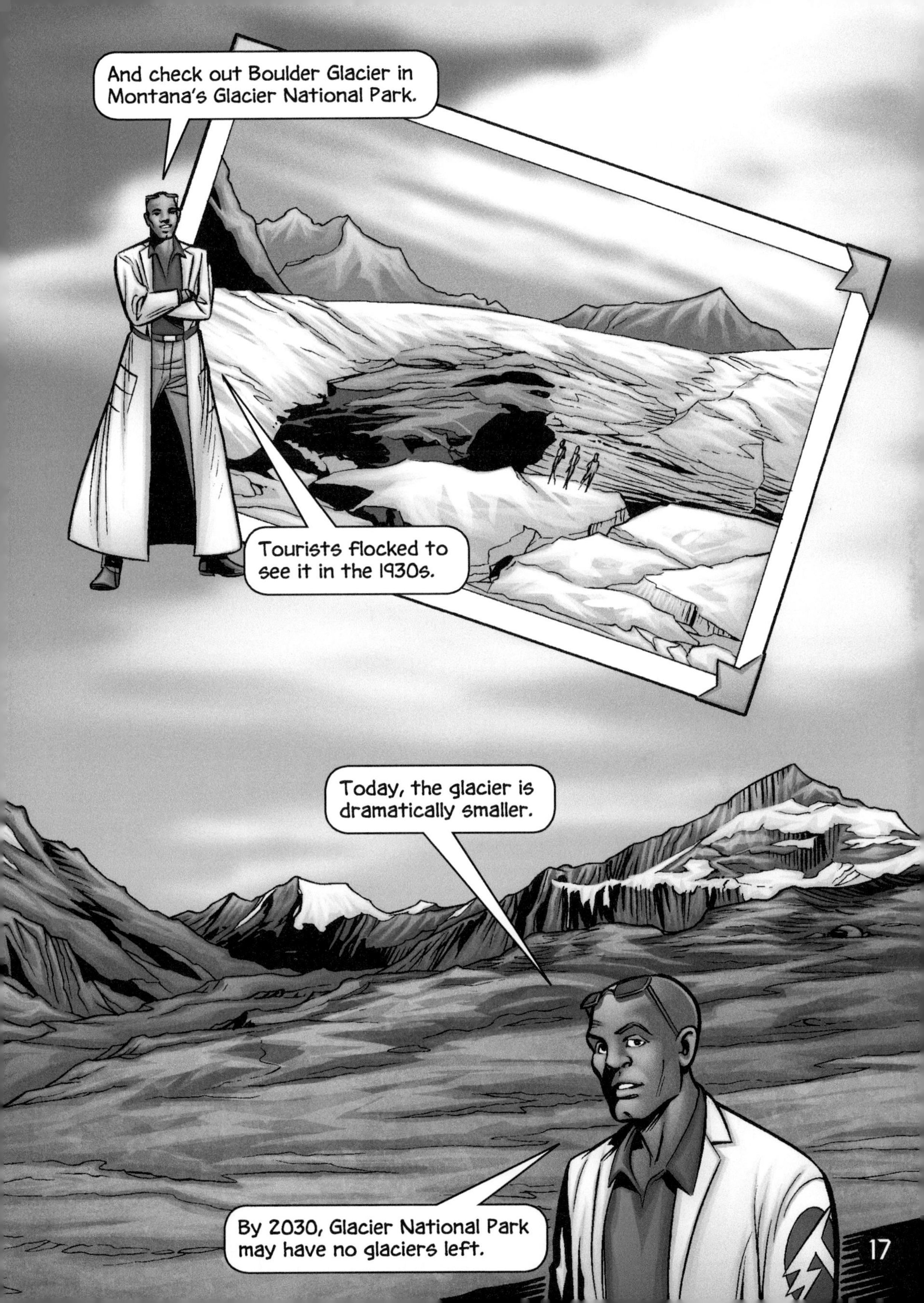
And check out Boulder Glacier in Montana's Glacier National Park.
Tourists flocked to see it in the 1930s.
Today, the glacier is dramatically smaller.
By 2030, Glacier National Park may have no glaciers left.

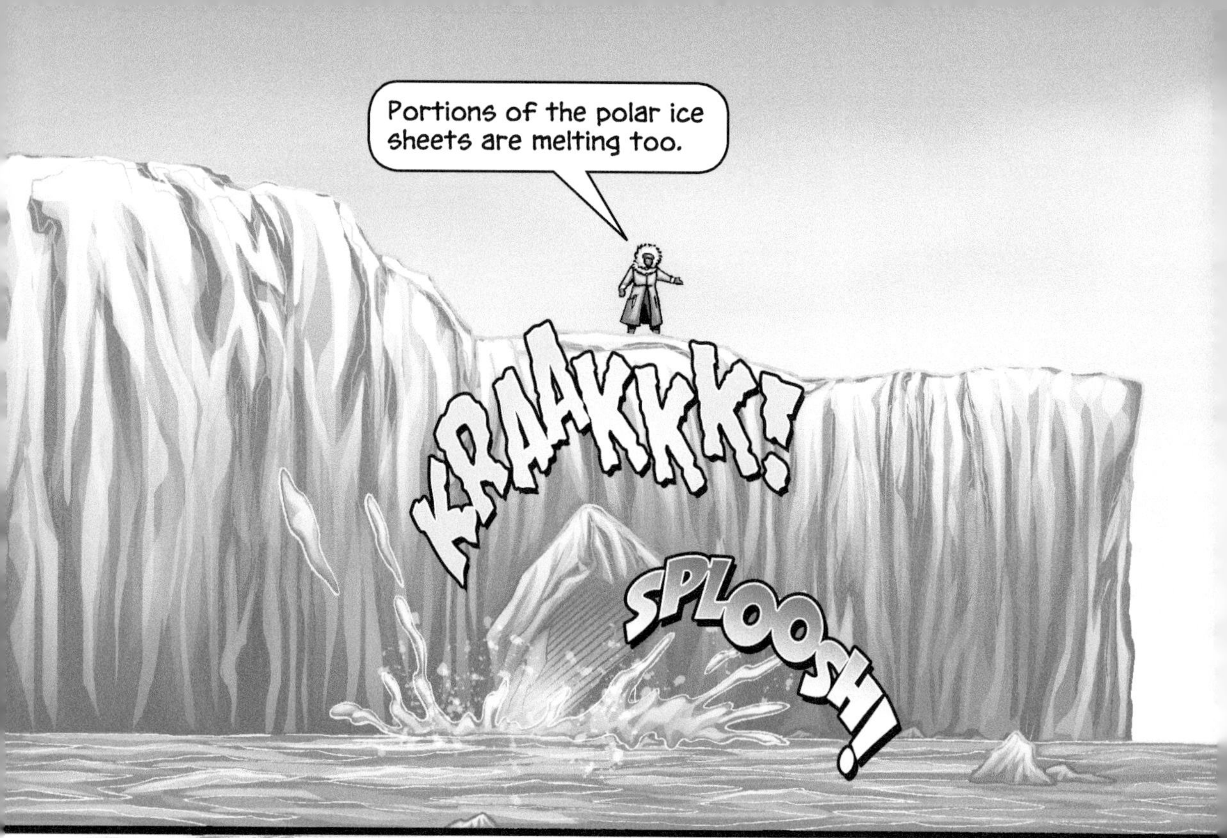
Portions of the polar ice sheets are melting too.
KRAAKKK!
SPLOOSH!

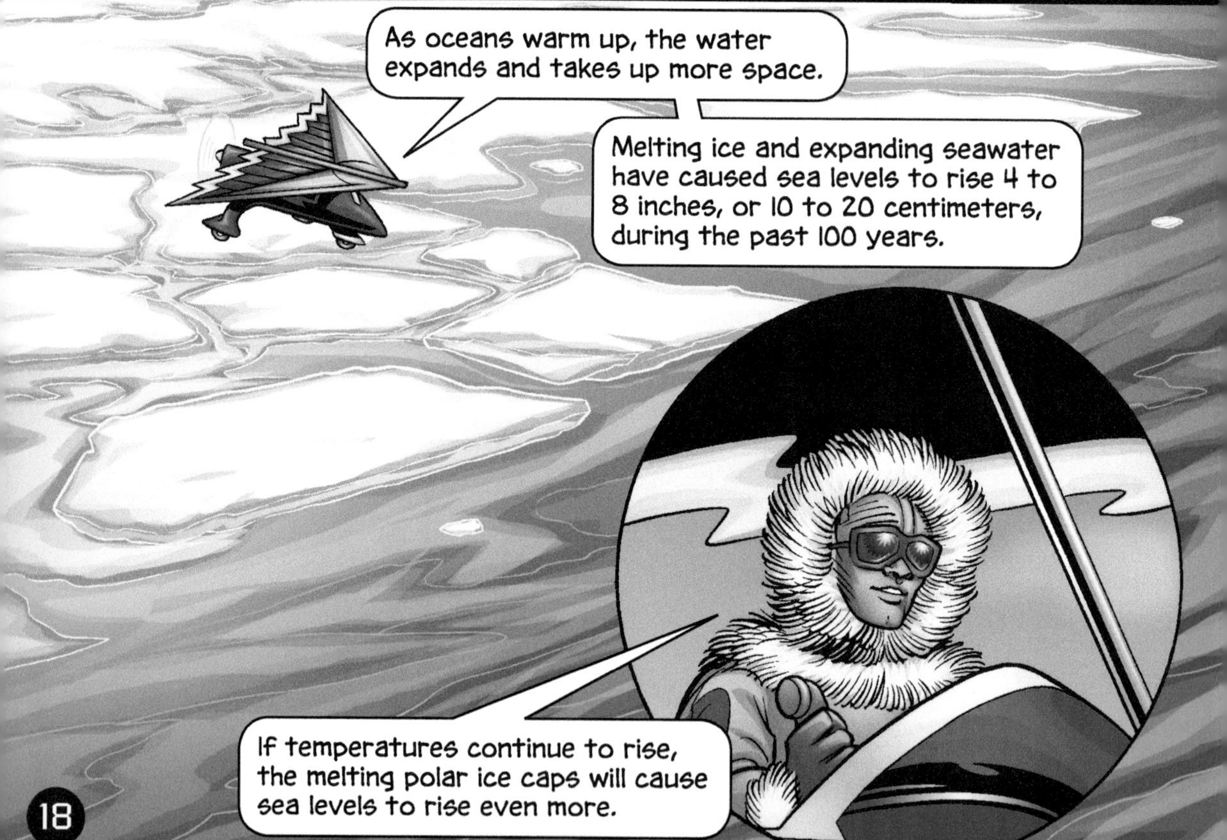
As oceans warm up, the water expands and takes up more space.
Melting ice and expanding seawater have caused sea levels to rise 4 to 8 inches, or 10 to 20 centimeters, during the past 100 years.
If temperatures continue to rise, the melting polar ice caps will cause sea levels to rise even more.

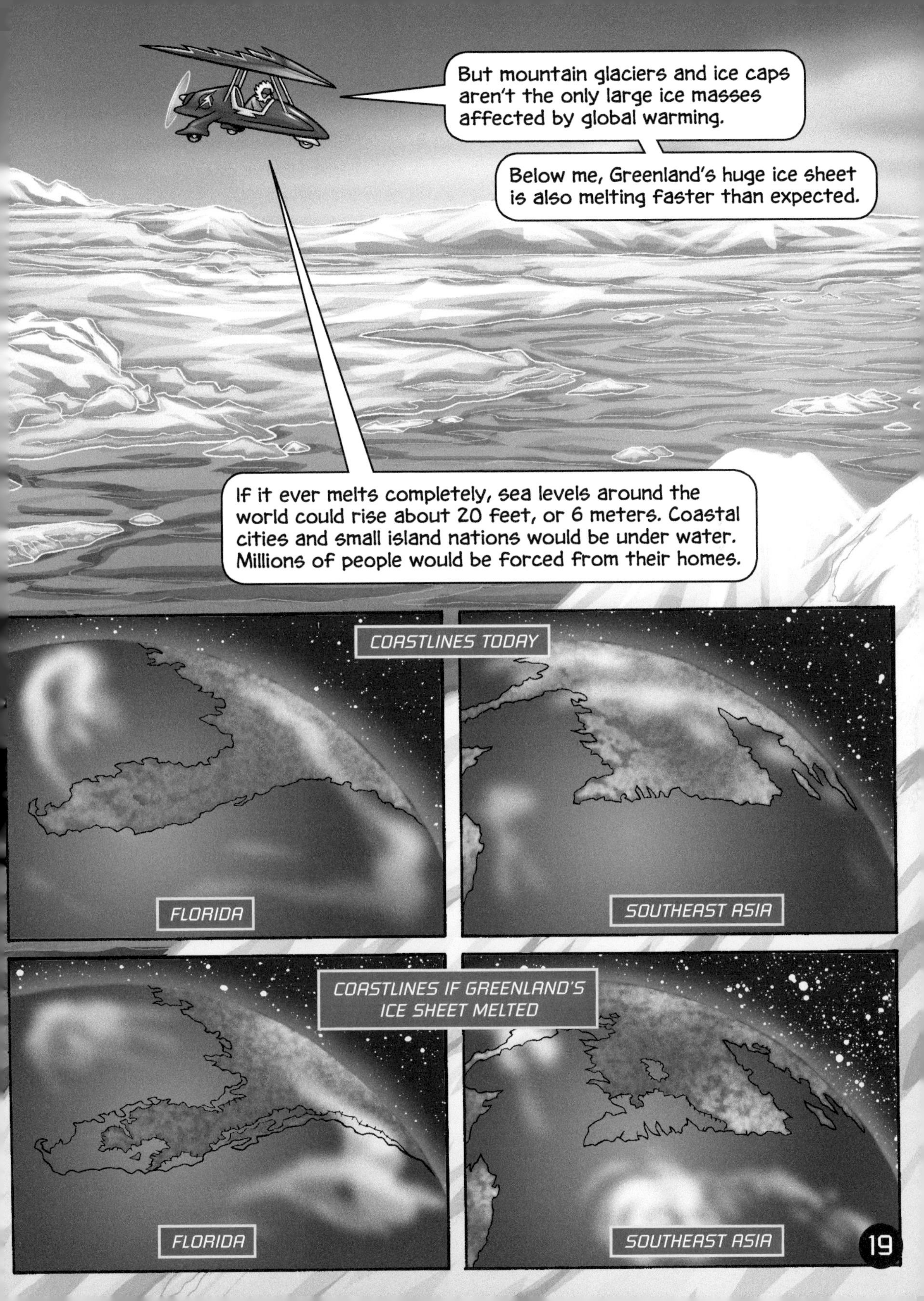
But mountain glaciers and ice caps aren't the only large ice masses affected by global warming.
Below me, Greenland's huge ice sheet is also melting faster than expected.
If it ever melts completely, sea levels around the world could rise about 20 feet, or 6 meters. Coastal cities and small island nations would be under water. Millions of people would be forced from their homes.
COASTLINES TODAY
FLORIDA
SOUTHEAST ASIA
COASTLINES IF GREENLAND'S ICE SHEET MELTED
FLORIDA
SOUTHEAST ASIA

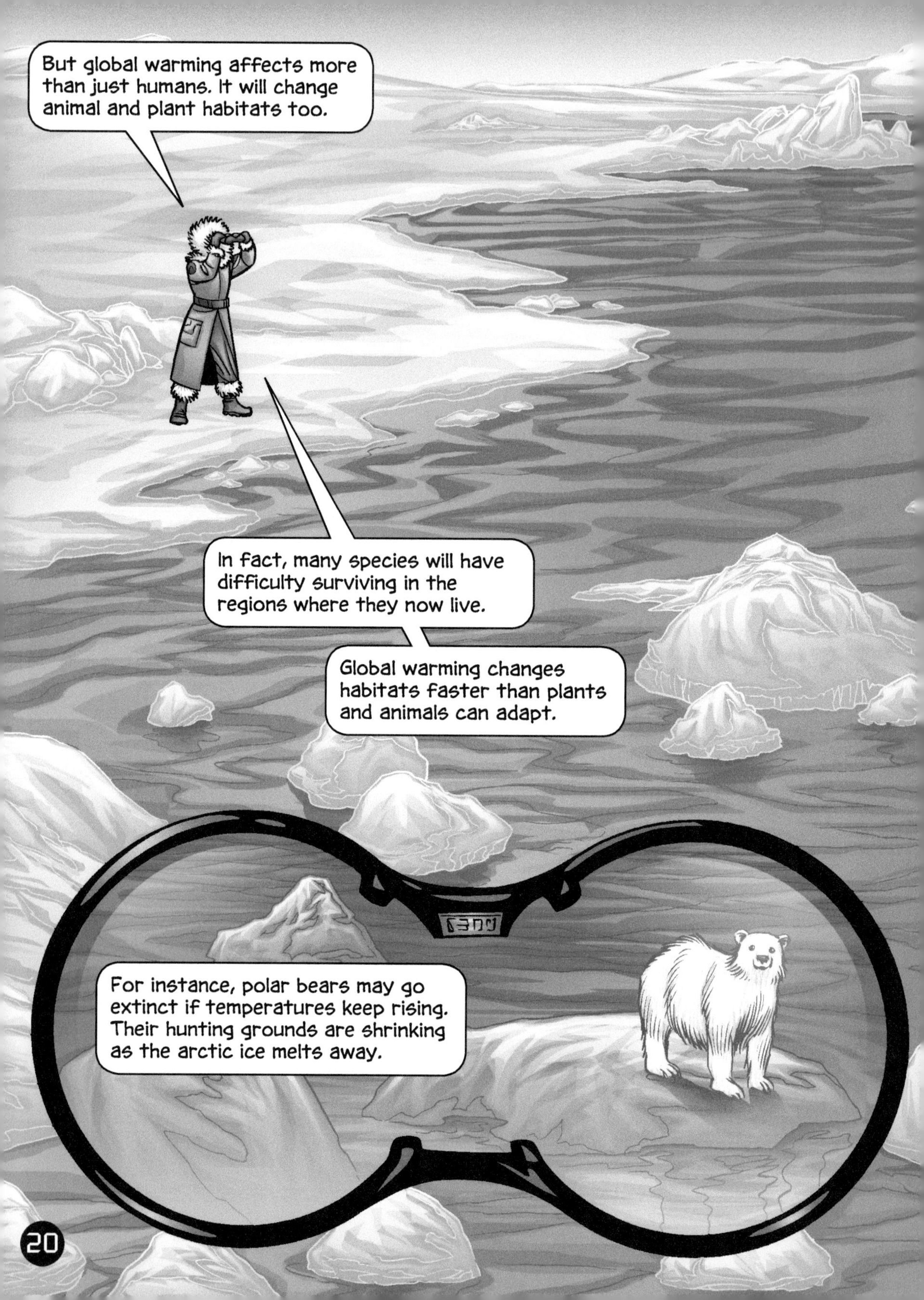

But global warming affects more than just humans. It will change animal and plant habitats too.
In fact, many species will have difficulty surviving in the regions where they now live.
Global warming changes habitats faster than plants and animals can adapt.
For instance, polar bears may go extinct if temperatures keep rising. Their hunting grounds are shrinking as the arctic ice melts away.

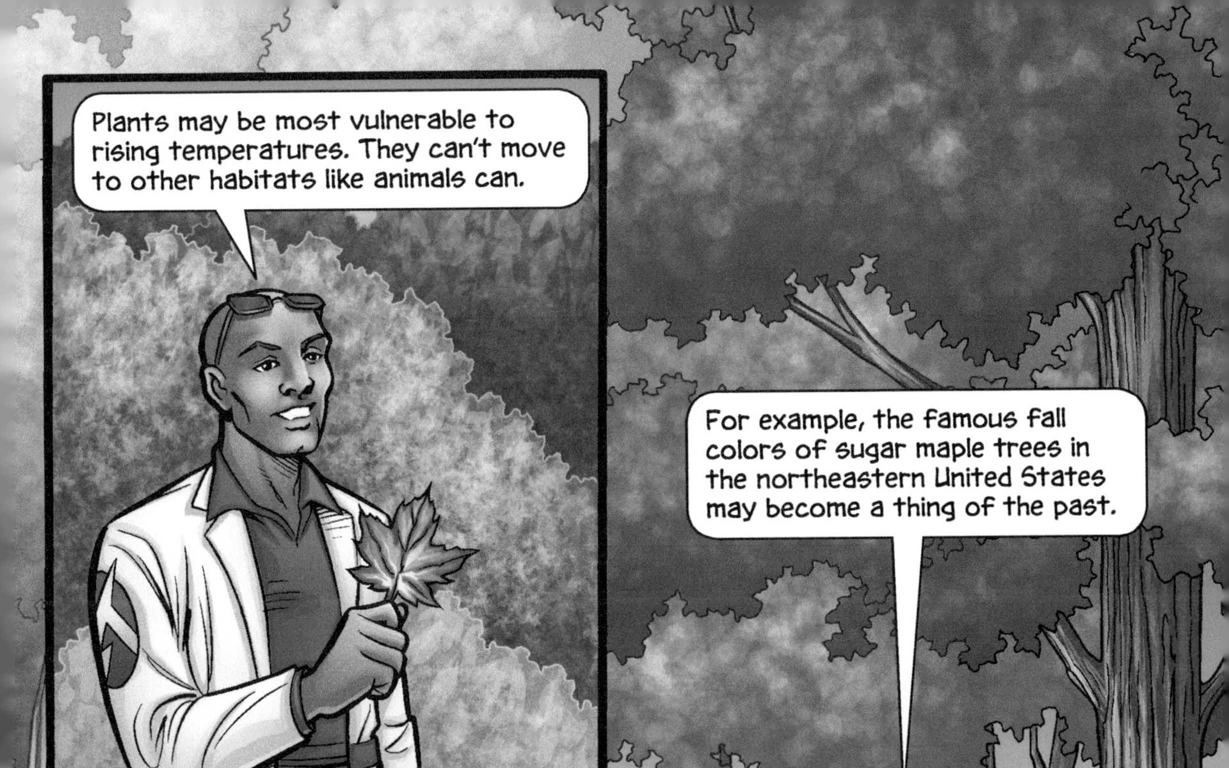
Plants may be most vulnerable to rising temperatures. They can't move to other habitats like animals can.
For example, the famous fall colors of sugar maple trees in the northeastern United States may become a thing of the past.
These beautiful trees need cooler temperatures to survive. They'll die out as global warming creates longer, warmer summers in this region.

AGRICULTURAL IMPACT

ACCESS GRANTED: MAX AXIOM

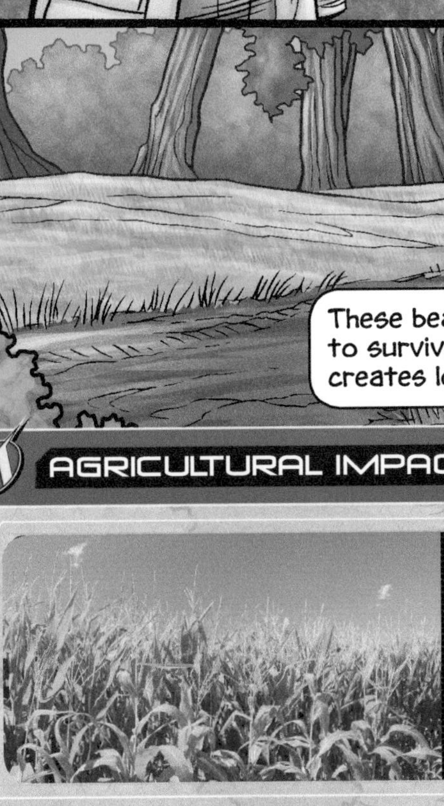

Global warming may benefit some colder regions such as Canada and Russia by creating a longer season to grow crops. At the same time, rising temperatures and droughts may destroy crops in warmer regions farther south.

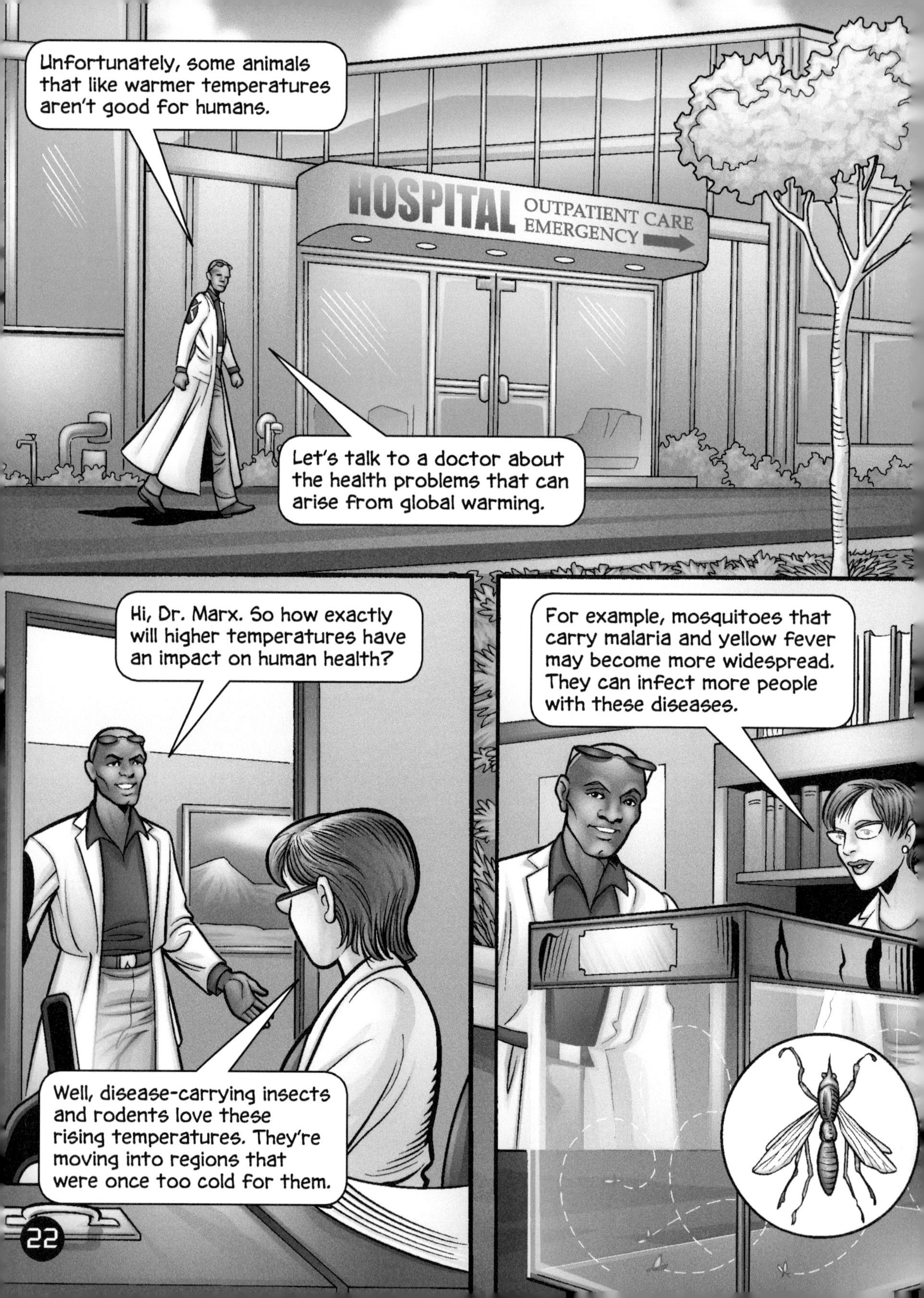

Unfortunately, some animals that like warmer temperatures aren't good for humans.
HOSPITAL
OUTPATIENT CARE
EMERGENCY
Let's talk to a doctor about the health problems that can arise from global warming.
Hi, Dr. Marx. So how exactly will higher temperatures have an impact on human health?
Well, disease-carrying insects and rodents love these rising temperatures. They're moving into regions that were once too cold for them.
For example, mosquitoes that carry malaria and yellow fever may become more widespread. They can infect more people with these diseases.

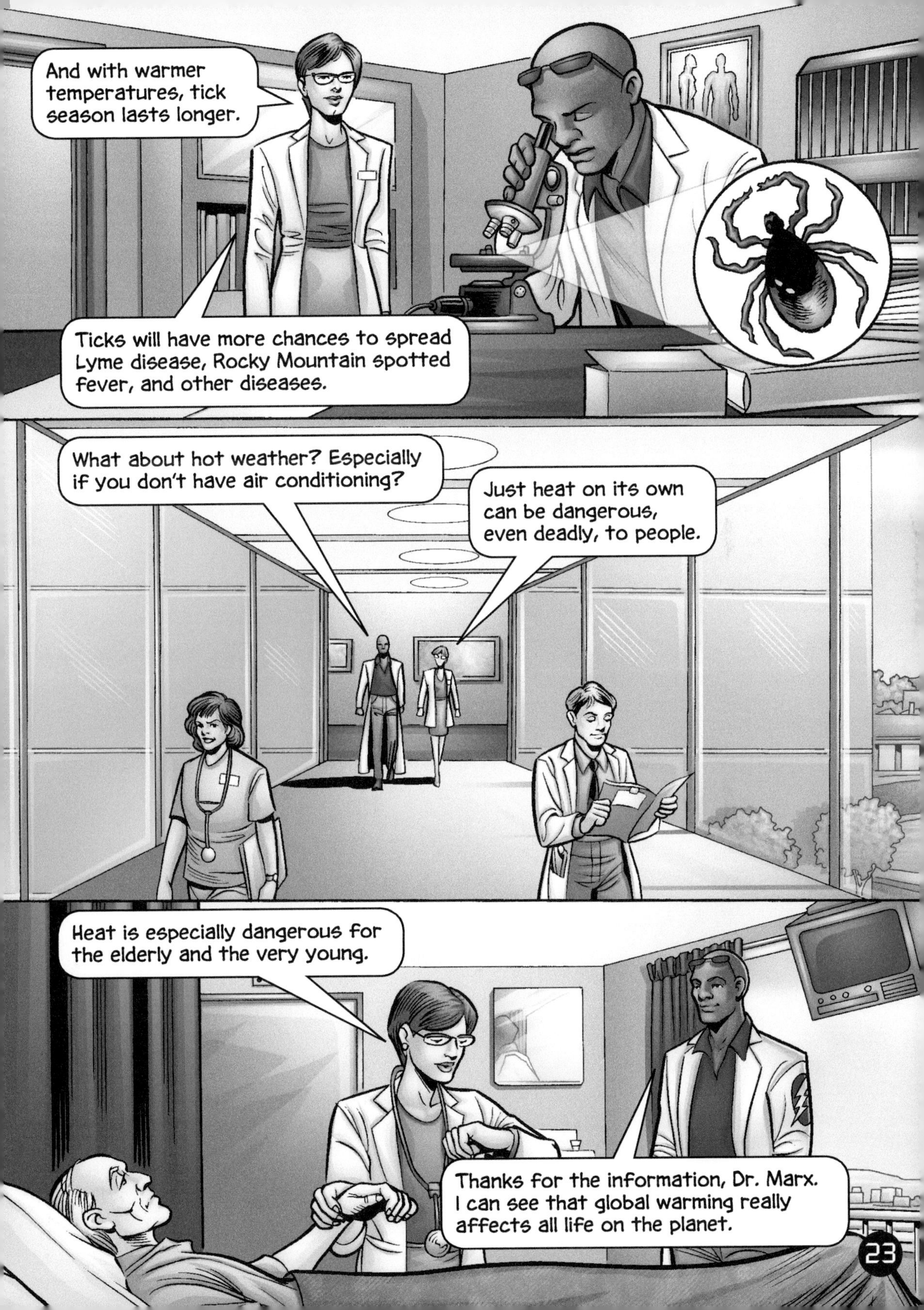
And with warmer temperatures, tick season lasts longer.
Ticks will have more chances to spread Lyme disease, Rocky Mountain spotted fever, and other diseases.
What about hot weather? Especially if you don't have air conditioning?
Just heat on its own can be dangerous, even deadly, to people.
Heat is especially dangerous for the elderly and the very young.
Thanks for the information, Dr. Marx. I can see that global warming really affects all life on the planet.

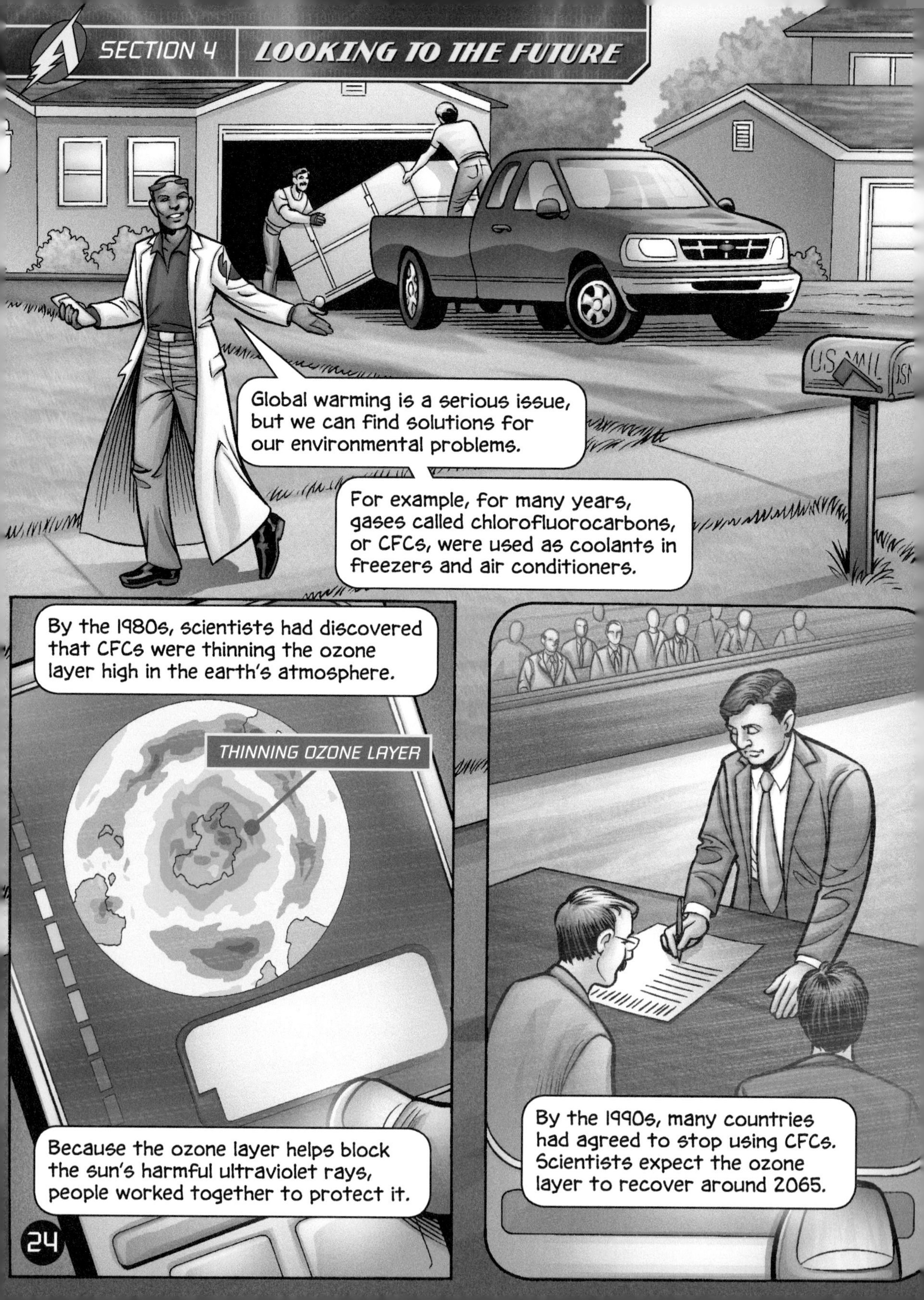
Global warming is a serious issue, but we can find solutions for our environmental problems.
For example, for many years, gases called chlorofluorocarbons, or CFCs, were used as coolants in freezers and air conditioners.
By the 1980s, scientists had discovered that CFCs were thinning the ozone layer high in the earth's atmosphere.
THINNING OZONE LAYER
Because the ozone layer helps block the sun's harmful ultraviolet rays, people worked together to protect it.
By the 1990s, many countries had agreed to stop using CFCs. Scientists expect the ozone layer to recover around 2065.

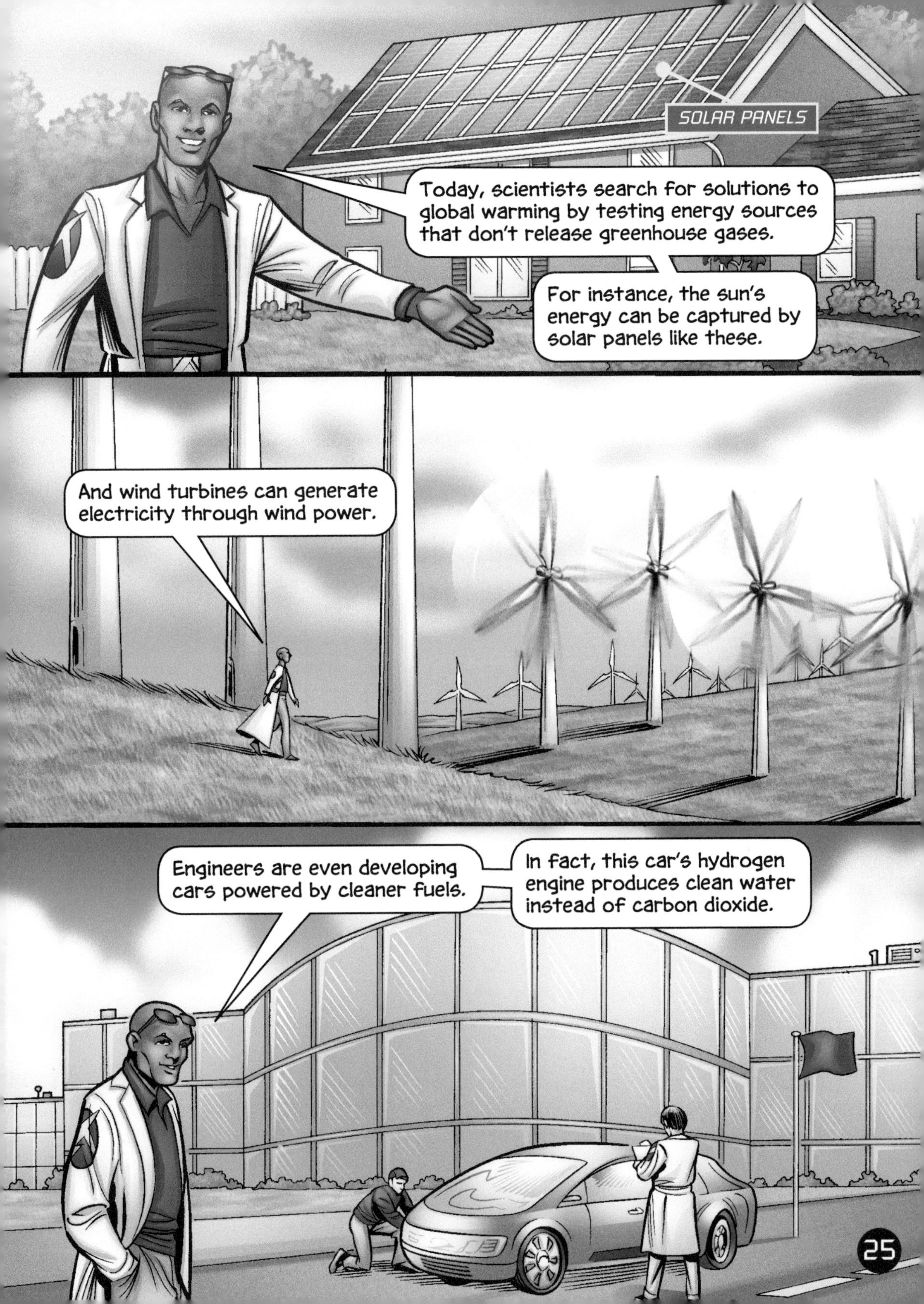
SOLAR PANELS
Today, scientists search for solutions to global warming by testing energy sources that don't release greenhouse gases.
For instance, the sun's energy can be captured by solar panels like these.
And wind turbines can generate electricity through wind power.
Engineers are even developing cars powered by cleaner fuels.
In fact, this car's hydrogen engine produces clean water instead of carbon dioxide.

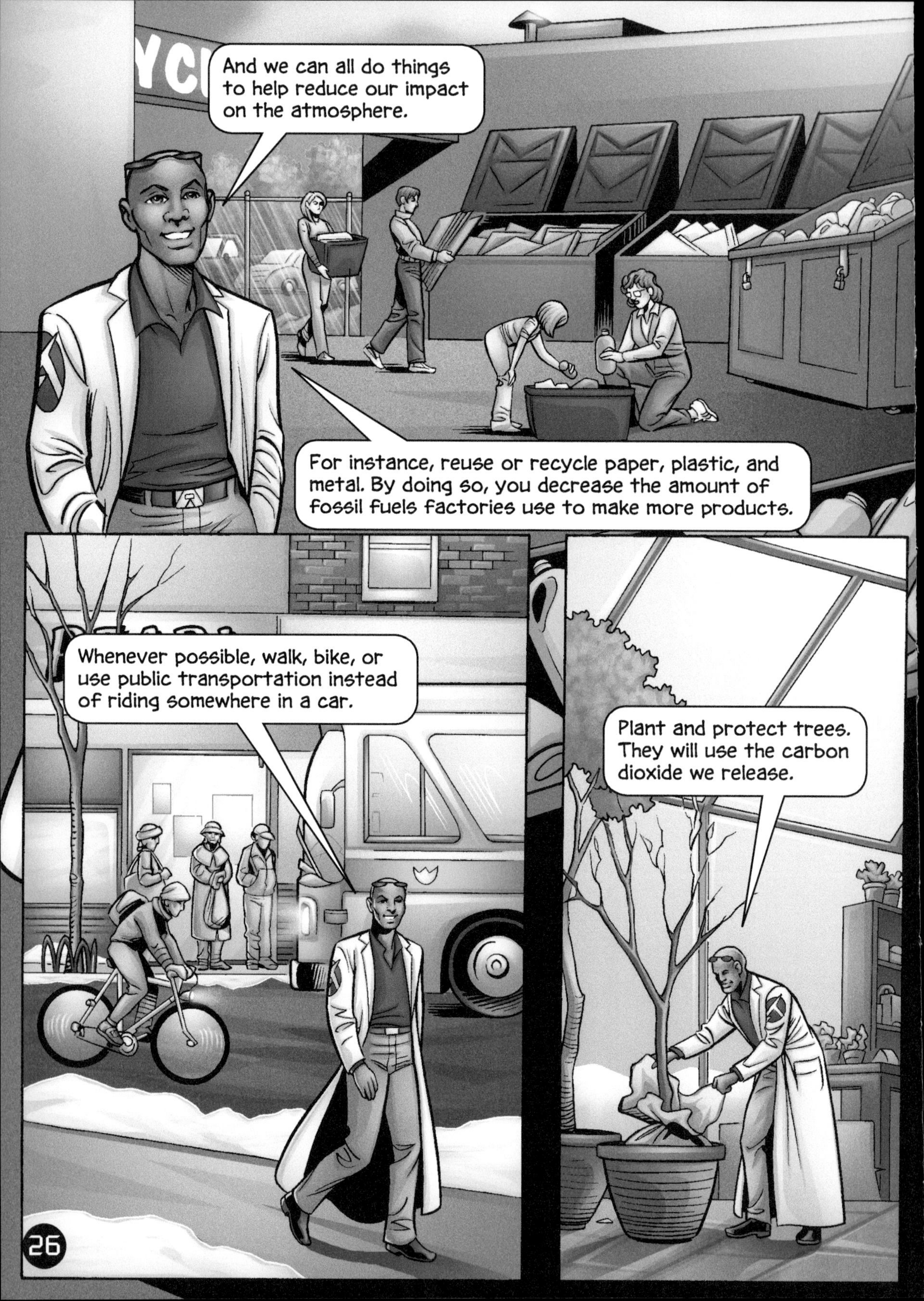
And we can all do things to help reduce our impact on the atmosphere.
For instance, reuse or recycle paper, plastic, and metal. By doing so, you decrease the amount of fossil fuels factories use to make more products.
Whenever possible, walk, bike, or use public transportation instead of riding somewhere in a car.
Plant and protect trees. They will use the carbon dioxide we release.

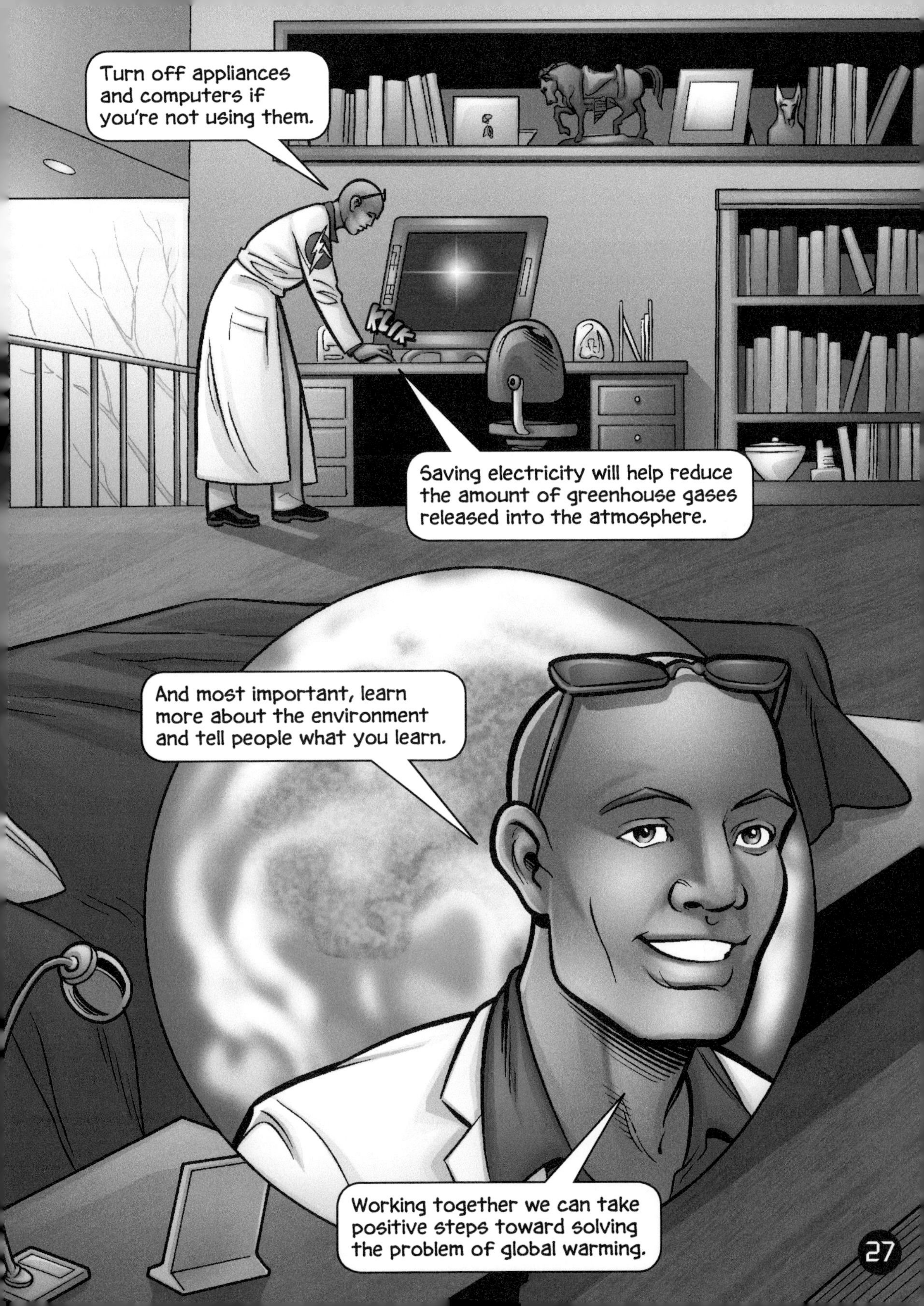
Turn off appliances and computers if you're not using them.
KLIK
Saving electricity will help reduce the amount of greenhouse gases released into the atmosphere.
And most important, learn more about the environment and tell people what you learn.
Working together we can take positive steps toward solving the problem of global warming.

MORE ABOUT GLOBAL WARMING

- Venus is the hottest planet in our solar system. Many astronomers believe its heat is due to a massive greenhouse effect. Carbon dioxide makes up a whopping 97 percent of Venus's atmosphere. The planet's thick clouds and dense atmosphere help trap the sun's heat, making Venus's surface temperature 870 degrees Fahrenheit (466 degrees Celsius). That's hot enough to melt lead!

- After carbon dioxide, methane is the greenhouse gas most produced by humans. Methane is released by landfills and is a by-product of coal mining. Believe it or not, cows are also a source of methane. When cows burp or pass gas, they release methane. As the demand for beef rises, more cattle are raised and more methane is released into the air.

- The United States is responsible for more greenhouse gas pollution than any other country in the world.

- Hurricanes have different names depending on where they occur in the world. If they appear on the Pacific Ocean, they're called typhoons. When they form on the Indian Ocean, they're called tropical cyclones.

- Ozone gas can be good or bad, depending on where it lies in the atmosphere. The ozone layer 10 to 30 miles (16 to 48 kilometers) high works as a shield to protect life on Earth from the sun's dangerous ultraviolet radiation. This radiation can lead to skin cancer in humans. Nearer the earth's surface, ground-level ozone is a health hazard, damaging lungs and hurting plants.

- The Arctic's sea ice is also melting quickly. Because snow and ice are white, the sea ice works like a big mirror, reflecting most of the sun's rays. As global temperatures rise, however, some of the ice melts. This melting reveals the ocean water below. Because the water is darker than the ice, it absorbs more of the sun's energy and warms up. The warmer water leads to even more of the sea ice melting, which leads to even more water being revealed. The cycle goes on and on.

- You've probably seen hybrid cars on the road or on TV. Hybrid cars run on both gasoline and electricity. Because they don't use as much gas as regular cars, they produce less pollution.

TEST THE WATERS

What happens to the world's oceans when sea—or land—ice begins to melt due to Earth's rising temperature? Build a simulation and find out!

WHAT YOU NEED:

- 2 empty and clean individual-serving yogurt containers
- water
- clean plastic paint pan
- sand or pebbles
- butter knife
- plastic ruler
- paper and pencil
- small cup

WHAT YOU DO:

1. Fill the yogurt containers with water and freeze overnight.

2. Cover the slope of the paint pan with sand or small pebbles. This section represents land.

3. Pour room-temperature water into the reservoir (the deep part) of the paint pan until it is about half full. This water represents the ocean.

4. Remove one yogurt container from the freezer. Use a butter knife to carefully remove the ice.

5. Add your ice to the reservoir. This ice represents sea ice.

6. Using the ruler, immediately measure how high the water comes up the side and slope of the paint pan. Record the measurements on a piece of paper.

7. On your paper, make a prediction about the water level. What do you think will happen when the ice melts?

8. When the ice is fully melted, use the ruler to measure the new water level. Record your measurements and compare them to your earlier measurements. What changed? Make any observations you notice.

9. Remove the second yogurt container from the freezer and take out the ice and place it on top of the sand or pebbles. This ice represents land ice, like a glacier.

10. On your paper, make a new prediction: what do you think will happen when the ice melts?

11. When the ice is fully melted, use the ruler to measure the new water level. Record your measurements and compare them to your first. What changed? Make any observations you notice.

DISCUSSION QUESTIONS

1. The use of fossil fuels contributes to global warming. How can people in your area reduce their use of fossil fuels to help slow down global warming?

2. What are at least five effects of global warming on our planet and its inhabitants? Which one do you think is the most harmful?

3. Discuss what you think will happen if temperatures continue to rise on Earth. Do you think rising temperatures are a good thing or a bad thing? Why?

4. How do changing temperatures have different effects on different people? Discuss who would be most strongly affected by heat waves and why.

WRITING PROMPTS

1. Humans have a major effect on global warming. List at least four human activities that contribute to Earth's greenhouse effect. Draw a picture to represent each activity.

2. What causes the thinning of Earth's ozone layer? Draw a diagram of the greenhouse effect.

3. Global warming can have effects even in your neighborhood. Write a paragraph explaining two effects global warming might have on your area.

4. Imagine it is the year 2100. Write a short news article explaining what effect global warming is having on Earth almost 100 years from now.

TAKE A QUIZ!

GLOSSARY

atmosphere (AT-muhs-fihr)—the mixture of gases that surrounds the earth

average (AV-uh-rij)—a common amount of something; an average amount is found by adding figures together and dividing by the number of figures.

carbon dioxide (KAHR-buhn dye-AHK-side)—a colorless, odorless gas that people and animals breathe out; plants take in carbon dioxide because they need it to live.

climate (KLEYE-mit)—the usual weather that occurs in a place

drought (DROUT)—a long period of weather with little or no rainfall

fossil fuels (FOSS-uhl FYOO-uhls)—natural fuels formed from the remains of plants and animals; coal, oil, and natural gas are fossil fuels.

glacier (GLAY-shur)—a huge moving body of ice found in mountain valleys or polar regions

habitat (HAB-uh-tat)—the natural place and conditions in which a plant or animal lives

ozone layer (OH-zohn LAY-ur)—the thin layer of ozone high above the earth's surface that blocks out some of the sun's harmful rays

photosynthesis (foh-toh-SIN-thuh-sis)—the process by which plant cells use energy from the sun to combine carbon dioxide, water, and minerals to make food for plant growth; photosynthesis releases oxygen into the atmosphere.

radiate (RAY-dee-ate)—to give off energy

READ MORE

Buchanan, Shelly. *Global Warming*. Science Readers: Content and Literacy Series. Huntington beach, Cali.: Teacher Created Materials, 2015.

Coutts, Lyn. *Global Warming*. Visual Explorers. Hauppauge, N.Y.: Barron's Educational Series, 2017.

Herman, Gail. *What is Climate Change?* What Was? Series. New York: Penguin Young Readers, an Imprint of Penguin Group Inc., 2018.

Mack, Molly. *Reducing Global Warming*. Global Guardians. New York: The Rosen Publishing Group, 2017.

INTERNET SITES

Use Facthound to find Internet sites related to this book.

Visit *www.facthound.com*

Just type in 9781543529531 and go!

Check out projects, games and lots more at
www.capstonekids.com

INDEX